Inviting Catholics Home

A Parish Program

Sally L. Mews

Liguori
LIGUORI, MISSOURI

Imprimi Potest:
Richard Thibodeau, C.Ss.R.
Provincial, Denver Province
The Redemptorists

Imprimatur:
Most Reverend Michael J. Sheridan
Auxiliary Bishop, Archdiocese of St. Louis

Published by Liguori Publications
Liguori, Missouri
www.liguori.org

Library of Congress Cataloging-in-Publication Data

Mews, Sally L.
    Inviting Catholics home : a parish program / Sally L. Mews.—1st ed.
        p. cm.
    Includes bibliographical references.
    ISBN 978-0-7648-0844-9 (pbk.)
    1. Ex-church members—Catholic Church. 2. Catholic Church—History—1965–.
3. Church work with ex-church members—Catholic Church. 4. Catholic Church—
Membership. I. Title.

BX2347.8.E82 M49 2002
269'.2'08822—dc21   20022018985

Liguori Publications, a nonprofit corporation, is an apostolate of the Redemptorists. To learn more about the Redemptorists, visit *Redemptorists.com*.

Printed in the United States of America
10   7 6

Inviting Catholics Home

*This book is dedicated
to the memory
of the late Alvin Illig, C.S.P.,
founder of the Paulist
National Catholic Evangelization
Association, who affirmed, encouraged,
and inspired me to follow his leadership
in ministry to inactive Catholics;
and to
my beloved husband,
Harvey F. Mews, Jr.,
who is my best friend, advisor,
lifelong companion, and
partner in everything, including
ministry to inactive Catholics.*

—Sally L. Mews

Table of Contents

~

Acknowledgments ix

Foreword xi

Preface xv

Introduction xix

CHAPTER 1:
    Why People Leave the Church and Why They Return 1

CHAPTER 2:
    Overview of Catholics Returning Home Program 9

CHAPTER 3:
    Basic Program Requirements for Catholics
    Returning Home 27

CHAPTER 4:
    Checklist for Starting a Catholics Returning
    Home Program 39

CHAPTER 5:
    Details of Six-Week Sessions 47

        Session #1: Welcome/Completion of Anonymous
                Questionnaires 47

        Session #2: Sharing Stories of Faith 61

Session #3: The Church Today: Changes Since
Vatican II 65

Session #4: The Mass 68

Session #5: Explanation of the Sacrament of
Penance/Confession 70

Session #6: Wrap-up, Evaluation, and Discussion
of the Creed 73

CHAPTER 6:
Follow-Up Sessions and Ongoing Support 81

CHAPTER 7:
Publicity 83

CHAPTER 8:
A Final Word of Encouragement 99

Appendix: Sources for Programming 101

Acknowledgments

~

Many thanks to:

Fr. William McKee, C.Ss.R., Liguori, Missouri, pioneer and forerunner in ministry to inactive Catholics.

Msgr. Thomas Cahalane, Tucson, Arizona, founder of "Alienated Catholics Anonymous."

Richard Pitre, M.Div., Th.M., PH.D. (Cand.), theological consultant, Kennebunk, Maine.

Dr. William Manseau, D.Min., pastoral counselor, Emmaus Insitute, Inc., Nashua, New Hampshire.

Mary Ellen McGuire, Evergreen Park, Illinois, proofreader and editorial advisor.

Archdioceses, dioceses, parishes, and individuals who have shared their knowledge and experiences in order to enrich this ministry.

Gerald F. Kicanas, Co-adjutor, Diocese of Tucson, Arizona; former Auxiliary Bishop of Arch(d) of Chicago, Illinois.

Fr. Joseph W. Kruszynski, O.F.M., Director of Evangelization, Arch(d) of Chicago, Illinois.

Marge Lukacs, Arch(d) of Chicago, Vicariate I, editorial consultant.

Foreword

~

A prominent theme in the gospels is journeying. Jesus goes here and there and invites his disciples to follow him. Sometimes they are fearful of where he is going and resist. If they walk with him they get to witness transformation in others. The blind begin to see, the deaf to hear, even the dead rise; and eventually they experience it for themselves.

One of the most powerful journeys in the gospels is that described by Saint Luke where he tells what happened to two discouraged disciples who were leaving Jerusalem on Easter Sunday after disbelieving other disciples who said that Jesus had risen from the dead following his crucifixion. They were going away from their shattered hopes and dreams in Jerusalem to the town of Emmaus, disappointed and sad, when a stranger came along and asked them what was wrong.

They stood still at his greeting and then—letting their sadness show—they poured out their broken hearts to him as he walked along the road to Emmaus with them. He listened carefully and then he explained all that had happened in ways that were acceptable and meaningful to them. Their hearts began to burn within them in his presence. Taking him into their friendship they began to share a meal with him and only then realized who he was. Their lives changed forever and they rushed to Jerusalem to tell their friends that Jesus was indeed risen and alive.

Sally L. Mews's Catholics Returning Home program and her

ministry to inactive Catholics provide just such a journey. It meets people where they are in their quest for their spiritual home. The Catholics Returning Home program is explicitly structured to be respectful of their turning-point experiences which involve the choices made and adult conscience-forming perspectives taken. Inviting the questers to tell their stories of faith shaken, hurts experienced, or needs not met is a welcoming embrace. That mode of greeting and the journeying conversational process which follows is an acknowledgment that this is a discipleship community of equals. All are invited to tell their unique stories, to be understood, accepted, and sustained in growth by the risen Lord Jesus through his presence in word, sacrament, and community.

In human development terms it is usually necessary to leave home in order to become one's own adult self. The Book of Genesis talks about leaving one's parents and establishing one's own household. As James Fowler and Lawrence Kohlberg point out, both faith and moral development require a process of going through stages in which one's own distinct appreciation of ways to relate to others and to God is based on going through changes of perspective and a consequent enlargement of horizons and reordering of responsibilities.

Bernard Lonergan, S.J., referred to these processes as forms of conversion or transformation. He spoke of intellectual, moral, and religious conversions which constitute the human person's spiritual journey into selfhood. For Lonergan, religious conversion was falling in love with God with one's whole heart and mind. Necessary preconditions which affect the nature of religious conversion are intellectual conversion by which we become more realistic in our approach to life and moral conversion in which we become motivated by values rather than pleasures.

Sally Mews's approach to a ministry to inactive and alienated Catholics is one which is respectful of these dynamic processes in a person's life. It values questioning. It has grown out of the seedbed of her own experience of Twelve Step community spirituality. There people share with one another their own stories of how they learned to base their life on values rather than appetites, to restore broken boundaries, and to discover new horizons through honesty and reliance on one's Higher Power in community.

From these perspectives it is apparent that the decision to leave the conventional practice of one's faith for whatever reason may have been part of one's own journey towards intellectual, emotional, and spiritual maturity. A decision to participate in a returning Catholics program may be seen as the beginning of a person's adult claiming of their spiritual heritage. Part of a person's reclaiming the wholeness of her/his life and its heritages may well involve the assistance of a pastoral counselor who can help address any lingering emotional or psycho-spiritual wounds incurred along the path of one's life. Such assistance could also help the transitional process of returning to the Church itself. A good resource is the American Association of Pastoral Counselors, whose contact information is listed in the Appendix portion of this book. May the Lord of the journey to Emmaus walk with all who read *Inviting Catholics Home: A Parish Program.*

WILLIAM J. MANSEAU, D.MIN.
FOUNDER AND PRESIDENT, EMMAUS INSTITUTE, INC.
NASHUA, NEW HAMPSHIRE

Inactive Catholics

~

In the early years of my priesthood I often wondered why Catholics left the Church. Was there something wrong with the Church? Something wrong with them? What were the real reasons?

As a Redemptorist missionary those questions bothered me. Then one night I was at a social function in St. Louis, Missouri. A man came up to me with a drink in his hand and said quite loudly: "Hey, Padre, I used to be a Catholic." I said: "How long has it been?" He said: "Twenty years." I said: "Have you ever thought about coming back?" He said: "Many times." I said: "Why didn't you come back?" He said: "Because no one ever asked me."

I asked him. He set down his drink and we talked. We talked for several days after that. He and his family came back.

Then I wondered what would happen if we asked the sixteen million Catholics in this country to come back. I didn't know. I asked my superiors if I could ask as many as possible. They said yes. I had thirty-two years in the priesthood and naively thought that I was well prepared to minister to them. It took me nearly a year to come to the full realization that more was happening in their lives than the obvious fact that they did not go to church. For eighteen years I went up and down the country asking. In face-to-face—sometimes, nose-to-nose—conversations (and confrontations), I quickly learned that there was a lot more involved than merely asking. There were almost as many reasons for leaving the Church as there were inactive Catholics.

The journey with them has been the most beautiful grace of my fifty years of priesthood. The inactives taught me more about God and people than I ever learned in the seminary. They showed me facets of the human condition that I never dreamed of. They often made me lift my hands to heaven and cry out: "How Great Thou Art!" God never gives up on his people. It's awesome. Like the Hound of Heaven, "He pursues them down the nights and down the days and down the arches of the years." My priestly vocation has been strengthened by seeing the love God has for his people.

I learned more about the faults and failings of priests and nuns than I cared to hear. These inactives I spoke with were inclined to tell it like it is, and I learned some very important facts from these people. Most of the inactives are very fine people, law-abiding, tax-paying, child-loving men and women. They have about the same faults, failings, and sins as any cross section of practicing Catholics. They have *not* lost the faith, even though many of them say they have. One in a thousand has lost it, if that many. It is about as easy to lose the faith as it is to lose one's skin. Once a Catholic always a Catholic.

At first I took their complaints about Church people, Church doctrine, and changes in the Church at face value. They made an eloquent case for the wrongs they had suffered. But slowly I began to realize that there was more to what they were saying than was readily apparent.

I started looking for statements behind their statements, statements unspoken. I soon realized there was something else that served as a major factor in their Church decisions. It was that life and love had not turned out the way they hoped they would. Personal unhappiness, personal failures, broken relationships, financial worries, and health scares had deeply influenced their relationship with the Church. Frequently, when they looked for someone to blame, they blamed the Church, for this reason or for that. They had been let down more by life than by the Church. This, of course, does not in any way excuse priestly and religious failures in their regard.

I have frequently wondered why Jesus did not entrust his Church to angels instead of to us, imperfect men. Maybe we priests are a good example of an old principle: "God writes straight with crooked lines."

I was on the road for eighteen years with inactives and have spent the past four years on the Internet. On the road I met with about ten thousand. On the Internet, six thousand and more visit me every year.

When I left the road a young, vibrant, and apostolic laywoman appeared, as if sent by God. Her name is Sally Mews and she has been working with the inactives for many years. She herself was out of the Church for a period of time. She can speak to the inactives better than I from her own pain-filled experiences.

Sally, married, one son, has a full-time job as the tax expert for a very large corporation. She spends her weekends on the road, with her husband, going from one diocese to another, setting up Catholics Returning Home, a program which she developed. It has proven to be an effective method of bringing many inactive Catholics back to the Church and is the prototype presented in this book that is more broadly titled *Inviting Catholics Home.*

In today's highly-complex, enormously competitive, fast-moving, TV- and computer-dominated society there is a lot of pain. People are hurting. Their separation from their church and their God adds to their pain. The compassionate Jesus who spent most of his time on earth healing, curing, and raising from the dead, is our model for reaching out to inactive Catholics.

It has been my experience that the parishes which reach out to the stray sheep are never the same. Neither are those individuals who work in this field. The compassionate and loving Jesus is our generous master. He does not let his workers in the field go unrewarded.

WILLIAM F. MCKEE, C.SS.R.

From a Nonpracticing Catholic to an Evangelist—With God Anything Is Possible

~

My ministry to nonpracticing Catholics was born out of my own anger and pain. I know firsthand what it feels like to be angry and to feel separated from the Church because I was in that position for many years. I never imagined in my wildest dreams that I would ever return to the Catholic Church, much less actually end up leading a ministry to invite others back!

I was born into a nonpracticing Catholic family that was plagued by alcoholism, illness, and poverty. Except for a couple of weeks of summer catechism, I had no contact with the Church. However, when I was in the fourth grade, my family relocated due to my father's job and my parents decided to enroll me, my sister, and my brother in a Catholic school because it was located close to our home.

The setting was the pre-Vatican fifties which meant black-and-white answers from the Baltimore Catechism. Since I had limited contact with the Church prior to attending the school, I had had no exposure to the Baltimore Catechism or the answers therein. I figured a "daily missal" had more to do with the space program and sputnik than with the Catholic Church. As a result, I received a lot of negative attention from peers and teachers alike.

In addition, my family's poverty prevented them from paying

full tuition for me and my siblings—a fact we were continuously reminded of. I vividly remember the shame and hopelessness of being held responsible for something at a young age over which I had no control.

I spent many years angry at the Catholic Church and searching for an alternative. I looked at many other religions and at times considered myself a nondenominational Christian. Eventually I started reading the Bible, though I didn't read it end to end. Rather, I concentrated on the psalms and the gospels. Throughout this process, I felt a profound sense of conversion. I especially identified with the gospel outcasts with whom Jesus was fraternizing.

I researched the origins of the Catholic Church and—after much prayer, discernment, and personal struggle—I realized I *was* a Catholic Christian. I also realized that the Catholic Church is made up of imperfect people who do make mistakes. So I returned to a Catholic church. However, I did so quietly since it seemed that no one noticed that I had been away or that I had returned.

When I returned to the Church in 1980, I discovered I had missed out on the Second Vatican Council. I didn't find the Church I had left. Instead, I found an incredible array of "ministries" and lay involvement. I felt a growing need to share the "good news" of all these changes with other nonpracticing Catholics. I felt called to reach out to those alienated, inactive Catholics—those people who felt as hurt and separated from the Church as I did when I was away for all those years. As a result I embarked on a path which resulted in the design, testing, and implementation of a program I call Catholics Returning Home. Now I am hoping that this book, *Inviting Catholics Home*, which communicates my program in outline form will provide the blueprint and starting point for many other programs everywhere.

Inviting
Catholics
Home

CHAPTER 1

Why People Leave the Church and Why They Return

≈

Peole leave the Church for many reasons. Some leave because of boredom, indifference, ignorance and misunderstanding of the basic beliefs of the Church, anger and hurt—real or perceived— caused by representatives of the Church, anger at God, and a variety of other reasons. Relatively few people leave because of theological differences. Most people leave or drift away during their high school or college years while they're struggling with life choices and searching for their own identity. These folks normally aren't particularly angry. Rather, they don't see the relevance of the Church to their own lives because they're focused on finding and preparing for their lifelong career and determining their direction and status in life. Others who leave as adults usually do so with some degree of anger, hurt, or disappointment. Many leave the Church simply because they move to a new area and never make the effort to find and join a new parish, or they join a new faith community where they feel more welcome or at home than they did as a Catholic. Some leave the Church when they marry someone from a different faith or someone without any religious affiliation. For many people, it is a very difficult life choice to make when choosing between a loving companion and a church community.

Recently I got a call from an eighty-two-year-old woman who said she had been watching the periodic placement of the sign, "Catholics Returning Home begins soon, call xxx-xxxx at Villa Redeemer Retreat House in Glenview, Illinois." She said she lived in the apartments right next to the Villa and had seen the sign off and on over the last few years. Each time she saw it, she knew it was meant for her. She said she had wanted to call but couldn't because she had made a promise to her husband when they married over fifty years ago that she would become a Methodist and would raise the children as Methodists. However, this time she could make the call because her husband had died three months ago. She said she loved her husband dearly, that he was a good and kind man, that they had had a wonderful life together, and out of respect for him she had kept her promise. But now she could come back to the Catholic Church. She attended a local Catholics Returning Home series and happily returned to her faith home.

Let Faith Take Its Course

Many parents are upset when their children no longer attend church and wonder what they can do to bring them back. The answer lies in nonjudgmental acceptance of their children's choices and renewed commitment to their own faith development. We can't make anyone else return to the Church (or do anything else they don't want to do for that matter!). We can pray for others and invite them to return, but ultimately the choice is theirs. We can focus on our own walk with the Lord and renew that commitment. If others observe our peace, security, joy, and love of the Lord, they are likely to be drawn to the same source. Faith is caught, not taught, and it can never be forced.

We can invite others and let them know they're always welcome to attend or return to the Church. However, the key is to understand the difference of making a nonjudgmental invitation versus becoming a pest, hounding or badgering someone else, especially one's own children. Sometimes it's hard for parents to accept their children as adults who need to stand on their own feet and make their own life choices. Many returnees have said they left the Church precisely because religion was "shoved down their throats" by their parents and so they rebelled as soon as they left home. If our Father in heaven allows us the freedom to make our own choices in order that we may learn, grow, and develop faith and strength of character in our own time frame and in our own unique way, than we as earthly parents must strive to do the same. Faith is made stronger when it's allowed the freedom to grow and develop rather than being forced or controlled.

I've noticed that when people return to the Church after a long absence, most are very guilt-ridden for not having passed their faith on to their children. They agonize over not properly preparing their children for life. In many cases their children are already grown and these parents berate themselves mercilessly for having failed in their parental duties. I make it a point to explain to them that they have an opportunity to make a significant impression on their children, other family members, and acquaintances by the change they make in their own lives. By concentrating on their own faith walk and reveling in their newfound peace and joy in the Lord, others can't help but notice such a change. Older children especially will notice such a change in their parents.

Many Don't Believe They're Wanted

Most nonpracticing Catholics eventually want to return to the Church because of major life events such as a family crisis, an illness, a marriage, births, deaths, job loss or success, and many other reasons. As people begin to mature and question the paradoxes of life, they begin to search for the stability and peace that only God can provide in the Church community. The saying that babies are among the greatest apostles rings true because new parents frequently come back to the Church in order to pass on their faith to their children. Among the more heartbreaking stories I've heard from those who have been away from the Church come from those parents who say they've baptized their own children because they know they're excommunicated and can't return but at least they want to save their children.

A middle-aged dentist called me and asked what he could do to have his new baby and other young children baptized and made part of the Church. He said that he knows he's excommunicated because he was divorced and remarried and he didn't get an annulment from his first marriage. He said he doesn't know where to start in coming back to the Church since he has been away from the Church for over twenty years. He said he prays the Our Father over and over, hoping that God is listening to him. Also, he mentioned that he himself baptized his children because he's so afraid of approaching the Church and he didn't want them to be punished because of his failures.

Most nonpracticing Catholics would prefer to return to the Catholic Church—however, they don't know how. They are afraid to approach the Church for fear of being rejected. To those on the outside of the Catholic Church, it is perceived as a closed system. Being on the outside of the Catholic Church and feeling unwelcome is a very lonely place to be. It's very difficult for nonpracticing Catholics to get their nerve up to make contact with the Church. Thus, for those involved in various points of entry within parish ministries such as the parish school, Rite of Christian Initiation of Adults (RCIA), baptismal preparation, and parish registration, it's important to keep in mind what it took for that returning Catholic to show up on their doorstep.

Nonpracticing Catholics are especially concerned about their status in the Church and many mistakenly think they have been excommunicated and are not allowed to come back. Some will turn to a Protestant church because of the evangelization efforts by many non-Catholic Christian churches and because most Protestant churches welcome and accept them. In fact, many Protestant churches "target" inactive/nonpracticing Catholics in their evangelization efforts. Thus, it is most important to extend a personal invitation from the Catholic Church to welcome nonpracticing Catholics back to the Church. They need to feel that the Church wants them back and will take them back without putting them through a lot of red tape. "Once a Catholic, always a Catholic—*if you want to be*" is a saying that I have coined for returning Catholics to assure them they are welcome.

Accepting Adult Returnees As They Are

Many nonpracticing Catholics are unfamiliar with even the most basic beliefs of the Church and are at only a beginning level of understanding of the Catholic faith. Even if they have been educated in the Catholic school system, most of those who have been away from the Church are very confused and mixed-up about Catholic beliefs. Even if they're highly educated and successful in life, many of these nonpracticing Catholics are truly children in adult bodies with regard to their understanding of the Catholic faith. It doesn't matter if they are doctors, lawyers, have Ph.D.'s, or are successful millionaires—many returnees are almost childlike when it comes to their concepts and ideas about the Catholic religion.

While presenting a Catholics Returning Home program in the Archdiocese of Atlanta, I had just explained my belief that many returning Catholics are at a grade-school level of understanding of the Catholic faith and that they even talk about faith and religion in the language of their childhood. Right after that part of the presentation, we took a short break and a priest came up to me and said that just the evening before he had an experience with a returning Catholic that embodied that very reality. The priest said the returning Catholic asked him a question about the Catholic faith that was so naive that he was amazed an educated adult would even consider such a question. So, to make a point, the priest asked the man if he as a forty-five-year-old man still believed and followed what his mother told him about sex when he was in grade school. His mother's teaching about sex in grade school was appropriate at the time, but certainly not for use as a mature adult. The priest told the man that it's the same with the teachings about the Catholic faith. The Catholic faith needs to be viewed through the lens of adulthood rather than understood at the grade-school level.

Returning adults are very sensitive and self-conscious about what they see as their lack of understanding of Catholicism. Thus, it's critical to present new information at a very basic level so that they don't become discouraged and give up. They desperately want to fit in and get "up to speed" and beyond their awkwardness. It's absolutely essential that all updates and handouts present information on a step-by-step basis at an understandable level.

Getting Up the Nerve to Come

One late October Sunday I went to Mass only to discover that daylight-saving time had occurred overnight and we forgot to change the time on our clocks. Thus, I arrived right in the middle of Mass. So, since I hadn't eaten breakfast, I went to a small diner a few blocks from the church. Because I was in a hurry and by myself, I took a seat at the counter. Next to me was a woman who—because the seats at the counter were rather close—kept rubbing elbows with me. This proximity opened up a conversation between us. I told her that I had forgotten to change my clocks and so I arrived late to Mass. She turned toward me, teary-eyed, and said with great emotion: "I used to be a Catholic but my parents stopped attending for years. My mother died a few months ago, but since we are excommunicated, we didn't have her funeral in a Catholic church. Instead, we had a small service in a funeral home and it was like burying a dog. It was awful and I'll never forget this experience for the rest of my life. I've been thinking about going back to the Catholic Church because the church down the street keeps putting a sign up that says 'Catholics Returning Home begins soon' along with a phone number, but I just haven't got the nerve up yet." I told her that I started that program and that she's more than welcome to attend. I'm not sure whether she came or not, but at least she was thinking about it and on the way.

Many people who have attended Catholics Returning Home sessions have said they attempted to come to earlier series, but were afraid to get out of the car. Instead, they sat in the parking lot. Others say they got lost on the church grounds trying to find the room where the meetings were being held. It's important to have signs up on the grounds and team members directing people where the meetings are going to be held. It is also very welcoming to people returning to have team members seeking them out and guiding them where to go. Many who call for information about Catholics Returning Home are very hesitant and fearful and some will say they're calling on behalf of someone else. Some attendees have said they're attending the sessions on behalf of someone else. It's important to accept everyone at face value and allow them their "cover" if that's what they need to feel comfortable in the group.

In one series, we had a man who regularly came to every single session, arriving early and staying late and participating with very great enthusiasm in the storytelling and sharing. However, during the first session, he said he was there on behalf of his wife because she was a fallen-away and angry Catholic and he was just trying to help her by attending since she had some scheduling conflicts and couldn't be there. At every session, he did a lot of talking and sharing, but prefaced every single comment with, "my wife would say this…" or "my wife feels this way…" or "my wife left because of.…" It soon became apparent that he was the real author of those comments. Even though he attended every one of the six sessions, he never changed his stance. He continued to be resolute that he was attending on behalf of his wife.

But all of this awkwardness, hesitancy, and fear displayed by returning Catholics is normal. It's all part of the process. The first step is often the most difficult for these people to make. I know what these people go through—what it feels like to be on the outside of the Catholic Church looking in—because I was a nonpracticing Catholic for many years.

CHAPTER 2

Overview of Catholics Returning Home Program

~

Origins

M y program for reaching out to inactive Catholics draws on Fr. William McKee's and Msgr. Thomas Cahalane's programs for reaching out to inactive Catholics, but it is primarily based on the methodology of the Twelve Step programs I have attended over the years. I have blended all these programs together with my own first-hand experience of being an angry, alienated Catholic and have developed a very simple, practical, parish-based process that is cheap, easy, and effective. The program that I outline here draws approximately ten percent of its material from Fr. McKee's program, twenty percent from Msgr. Cahalane's program, and seventy percent from my own personal experience of Twelve Step program methods and of being away from the Church and returning.

Fr. William McKee of St. Louis, Missouri, produced a video entitled "Inactive Catholics: Why They Leave…Why They Return" that I used to use during the second week of the series until I produced a new video entitled "Stories of Faith From Catholics Returning Home." The video includes testimony of actual returning Catholics sharing their stories of being away from the Church and returning. It is a very effective witness to returning Catholics to hear other people's faith stories. A picture is worth a thousand words and music touches the heart and soul in ways that words cannot. The imagery of the church scenes and the background music convey a hospitable welcome from the Catholic Church community in an effective, emotional manner. In addition, the returnees are impressed that "the Church" and in particular bishops, priests, and other laypeople care enough to create such a video just for them.

Msgr. Thomas Cahalane of Mother of Sorrows parish in Tucson, Arizona, developed a program called Alienated Catholics Anonymous in which he conducts an outreach process at Christmas and Easter to invite those who attend church only a couple of times per year to attend a six-week update on the Catholic faith. After the sixth session, he has the attendees from the prior series host a "Prodigal's Banquet" for the graduates of the current session. He also invites the current graduates to participate in the next outreach.

The Catholics Returning Home program is primarily based on my own experiences in various support-group programs, group therapy, and my actual journey back to the Church. I've attended Adult Children of Alcoholics (ACOA) group meetings for many years. The ACOA meetings are tremendously affirming, and it is healing to meet with others who have lived through similar traumatic experiences. It's much easier to open up and share with others who have been there and walked in your shoes because you're among peers. By being with peers who have also been wounded and traumatized, it allows one to finally trust enough to open up and feel, express, and verbalize the hidden shadows of the past. Listening to others' stories allows one to gradually identify, accept, and let go of pent-up rage, hostility, and pain. Having the ability to listen without being forced to participate allows one to regain trust and a sense of control and stability in order to face the unnamed terrors and fears that were denied and buried in the past during the actual trauma. By gradually unraveling the layers of hurt and anger, one is able to let go of those prior experiences and move on to healing, growth, and happiness.

During my years of attending Adult Children of Alcoholics meetings and Al-Anon (a support group for relatives of people suffering from alcoholism), I observed that most people who have lived through the dysfunction and trauma of alcoholism within the family abandoned the practice of their religion. Most stressed families become so traumatized and dysfunctional due to the addiction to alcohol or drugs that their lives become chaotic and disordered to the point that certain normal activities, such as attending church, are discarded. It is fitting, therefore, that the first step in the path toward recovery in Twelve Step programs is to re-establish a connection with one's higher power or God and eventually to some type of organized religion.

During my struggle to reconnect with my higher power or God, I found it to be very difficult to relate to much of the religious symbolism concerning images of God and family. If your natural father is abusive, violent, and cruel, it's very difficult to imagine a loving, caring, and kind God who is "father." Much of the religious imagery associated with the Church talks of a loving, forgiving family life—which is the exact opposite of the dynamic of an alcoholic family. If your mother, father, sisters, and brothers are angry, hostile, spiteful, and vindictive amongst themselves and to others, it's almost impossible to imagine a God or faith community that is loving and forgiving. If you're brought up to be shamed, chastised, and constantly told that you're worthless from early on in life, it's almost impossible to change your self-concept to one of self-love and acceptance. If your family of origin has been chaotic and abusive, it's difficult to develop trust in a church family.

Thus, a person who grew up in a dysfunctional family is at a severe disadvantage in learning to trust and belong to a faith community. As part of the Twelve Step process, one is encouraged to rely on the group itself as their faith community because most twelve-steppers are totally adrift and removed from any sort of organized religion or personal faith. Most of these folks are truly destitute, spiritually needy, and barely hanging on to any sort of spiritual connection. They are truly the poorest of the poor in their faith life and in their connection to organized religion. The abuse of alcohol or drugs has wreaked havoc and ravaged their family life and plunged most of these people into despair.

This same condition of alienation exists where other types of abuse such as incest have occurred. People coming from these types of families are deeply troubled and spiritually destitute. Dysfunctional families are very common. There are no perfect families. So many people have been affected by alcoholism in their families. As I've traveled all over the country leading Catholics Returning Home seminars, I'm always amazed at how many people tell me that they come from a dysfunctional family. It is important to remember, when conducting the Catholics Returning Home program, that many people returning to the Church have some type of dysfunction in their family which they are attempting to deal with in their adult lives.

What I really like about the entire Twelve Step process is that it's geared to accept people where they're at, no matter how destitute or hopeless they may be. There is hope for everyone no matter how bad the situation because people can always seek and gain the grace of God as they strive to change and improve. In the gospels, Jesus accepted people wherever they were spiritually or psychologically, but he always called them to more. He didn't turn anyone away who seemed lost or too far-gone. He purposefully sought out the outcasts, sinners, and rejects from the organized religion of his day. He was criticized and ridiculed for spending his time with such people. He offered them forgiveness and hope no matter what they had done. Thus, any program that seeks to encourage Catholics to return to the Church should be modeled after Jesus' invitation to and acceptance of all, no matter what they've done or not done—because no one is beyond the mercy of God. Jesus walked amongst known sinners and welcomed them back—we as his disciples can do no less.

Cheap, Easy, and Effective

Since I have developed and refined this Catholics Returning Home program over time based on trial and error, I have modified and reworked it to include what is absolutely the bare minimum requirements so as to accomplish the objective of helping people return and reconnect to the Church. As I have said, the program I have developed for returning Catholics is "cheap, easy, and effective." Every step and component part that I have kept in the program meets those three requirements. As I streamlined this program over the years, every step was measured and evaluated by those three criteria to be certain the program remained productive and accessible. By following the basic structure as I've designed it, the Catholics Returning Home program will serve your parish as an effective method to invite and welcome back inactive Catholics and help them reconnect to the faith community.

Before adding to or embellishing the basic program, the team responsible for implementation needs to consider the consequences of making the process more complicated and difficult to administer. Some parishes have actually stopped offering programs for returning Catholics after they added on so many enhancements and embellishments. These "extras" made the program too cumbersome and time-consuming that eventually the team burned out from attending to so many details. Keeping the program simple is the best for all concerned. Team members are frequently juggling family, work, and church responsibilities, so it's really important to minimize the time spent on meetings and preparation work.

In every parish where I've personally conducted a Catholics Returning Home program, I've kept to the bare essentials because I'm spinning too many plates to worry about too much detail. I've tried having coffee, soda, and cookies available, but I've always discontinued offering snacks and beverages because it was one more thing to do and I didn't view offering these as essential. The meeting time goes by so quickly and the interaction is so animated, emotional, and intense that most folks don't take time to eat and drink. If your team views offering drinks and snacks as essential, that's fine as long as it doesn't become so burdensome that it interferes with the effectiveness of the core mission.

Another optional addition is whether or not to have prerecorded background music. I've tried it, and it can enhance the mood, but it is not essential. It can become "just one more thing to do." Therefore, I usually don't provide background music. At my current parish, the choir practices the same night as the Catholics Returning Home program is held, so that attendees can enjoy the beautiful singing of the parish choir while I reserve my energies for the core of the program without being overwhelmed by details. And this specific scenario is probably better than bothering with prerecorded music because it allows returnees to experience the ongoing life of an active, vibrant church community along with enjoying the music.

One parish team met for months prior to launching a program for returning Catholics. They wanted the experience to be perfect for all involved. Every detail had to be meticulously planned. The team decided they had to have a special rug designed and created and placed outside the church doors. They labored over the color, texture, size, and the wording and symbols on the rug. One of the team members felt so strongly about the need for the special rug that she donated two hundred and fifty dollars to pay for the actual cost of the rug! In addition, the team wanted special invitations to be handed out at the Christmas Mass. The paper had to be of a specific texture and color. The fold had to be distinctive. The ink had to suit the paper perfectly. Then there was all the details to be worked out concerning hospitality and greeters. Surely, the greeters should all wear the same color clothes. And of course, there had to be special cookies and beverages. After all, if we're bringing people home to the church, everything must indeed be homey and homemade! So team members busily baked homemade treats, arranged place settings, and coordinated their attire. After all their planning and preparation, they launched their first series and had a great turnout of over twenty people. The series went well and they repeated it after Easter. In between each series and the individual sessions, the team met and evaluated and planned some more. However, by the third presentation of the series, they began to tire of all the meetings and planning and started to burn out. After even still more planning meetings, they decided that they just couldn't keep up with all the planning and administration entailed, so they discontinued offering the program.

Due to the constraints in most church budgets, I purposely selected and retained only the most inexpensive but effective means and methods of implementing a program for returning Catholics. For example, I recommend using "free publicity" in the religion section of the newspaper—rather than paid ads—in order to minimize the ongoing publicity costs. The wording I suggest on the outdoor signs doesn't include the specific dates so that the signs can be used again and again. The wording I prefer is: Catholics Returning Home program begins soon, call xxx-xxxx, St. Patrick's.

The methods that I have retained in the program "work" in the sense that inactive Catholics are invited back and reconnected to the Church. Some folks have asked what is the "success rate" of Catholics Returning Home. I would counter by saying what is the value of one person coming back to the Church? How can we measure the change in that person's life or the contribution that one person makes by being an active member of the community? Most of the returnees come back and reconnect to the church over time *if* they're treated in a kind and compassionate manner. The best way to evaluate the success of any program for returning Catholics is to marvel at the changed lives of those who do come back.

In my experience, we've had a very low drop-out rate in the actual sessions because we made a point of getting to know the returnees individually, talking with them after the sessions, calling them and trying to make them feel comfortable about joining our group and our parish community. Usually, those who dropped out of the sessions had some scheduling conflicts that interfered with their attending the complete series. However, many would return to later series. Some would attend off and on for years because they felt comfortable and at home with our group. Thus, if a particular Catholics Returning Home group is experiencing a high drop-out rate or if the returnees aren't staying or connecting with the Church, it's important to evaluate how welcoming and accepting your team is. Take a good look at how returnees are being treated. Ask yourself if you would want to join this particular group or parish community.

Frequently those who do return to the Church by way of this

program get very involved in ministry to other Catholics who wish to reconnect with the Church or in other activities within the parish. In my experience, most do come back eventually. It's best to let returnees proceed in their own time frame without undue pressure. A ministry to inactive Catholics is one of those rare efforts within the Church that continually attracts new team members and regenerates its ministerial team. Most other ministries in the Church are run by the same small group of "worn-out" people in a particular parish. However, Catholics Returning Home brings people back who have been totally disconnected and then allows them to become team leaders and to use their experience of being away to help themselves and others return to active membership.

A Ministry of Compassion

A ministry to Catholics who are returning to their faith is one of compassion rather than law. Jesus was a tremendously compassionate person. He refused mercy to no one. He put people first over law. When deciding whether to heal someone on the Sabbath or to be concerned about following the law, he chose to put people first by healing the person in need. He remained on the side of compassion. How do we apply Jesus' teaching to our modern-day Catholic Church and specifically to Catholics who are in the process of returning? Can we invite people back to the Church if they're living in situations that are at odds with Church law? It's one thing to talk about Jesus and quote Scripture and quite another to deal with the realities of Church law.

The answer is always compassion first. All of us are sinners and have fallen short of perfection. The Church is filled with sinners, so we always have room for one more! Only God can judge us and read our hearts and souls. We are called to commit others to the mercy of God who alone knows them and loves them with a father's love. If Jesus, the Good Shepherd, leaves the ninety-nine and searches out and seeks the one who has strayed and brings that one back to the flock, how can we turn that person away? If the very angels in heaven are rejoicing over the return of that one, shouldn't we be doing the same?

Frequently, team members are concerned about the status of the divorced who have remarried and they wonder how can we invite them back to the Catholic Church. Very simply, everyone is welcome to return and attend Mass and prayer services. People living in second marriages should be referred to the annulment/divorce ministry within the parish to work through their particular circumstances. In the meantime, however, they're welcome to attend the Catholics Returning Home program and other ministries within the parish. In speaking with returnees who have been divorced and remarried, one must be gentle and sensitive when discussing their status with them. I tell them that all the Church laws and rules are still in place but there is nothing they can't work through with the help of the Lord.

Catholics Returning Home sessions can be likened to the emergency room of a hospital in that content should be kept at a more general level to meet the needs of the entire group. For specific needs such as individual help with annulments, bereavement, or other issues, those folks should be routed to the various specialized ministries within the parish. In conducting a Catholics Returning Home program, you will need to know the channels—offices, names, phone numbers, addresses—to route people in their discussing the specific circumstances of divorce/remarriage/annulment and bereavement with a knowledgeable and caring representative of the Church. Based on my experience, there are some identifiable subgroups of returnees: about thirty percent of the returnees are concerned with divorce/remarriage; about twenty-five percent are grieving because of the death or illness of loved ones; and while most returnees are disillusioned or somewhat disenchanted with the Church, only a small number are really intensely angry or hostile.

Another subgroup of returnees is former religious which includes former seminarians, sisters, brothers, and resigned priests. While the majority of former religious are able to successfully move back into secular life and maintain a good relationship with the Church, some are not. Many of the former religious I've encountered in my ministry to returning Catholics were troubled, abandoned, and alienated. For some reason, these folks fell through the cracks and became alienated and adrift from the Church. Most of them wouldn't identify themselves as former religious in the group. They would only identify themselves as such in private, one-on-one meetings or telephone conversations. Some said programs for returning Catholics weren't for them because the Church doesn't really want them back. Some asked if there was room in the Church for a former religious. Many have shared pain-filled stories of being ostracized and mistreated by their families and others within their religious communities for leaving religious life.

Because they frequently aren't comfortable identifying themselves as former religious and sharing in the group, I searched for Church-sponsored resources and support groups for these former religious and was unable to find any. I did find a like-to-like ministry called WEORC (pronounced "work," it is the Old English spelling of that word) which is a nonprofit organization formed by Marty Hegarty, a resigned priest from Chicago, in the early 1970s in order to help former religious get jobs, offering counseling and support as well. I recommend referring any former religious to WEORC (for contact information see Appendix, page 104) so that they can find support from others who are in the same situation. Most of the former religious that I've met are faith-filled, committed disciples who are serving the Lord in various capacities. One can sense a holiness and goodness about them even though they're no longer formally in religious life. They are special, gifted, and good people who need and deserve our Christian love, compassion, acceptance, and understanding—never our harsh judgment and condemnation! They are our sisters and brothers in the Lord who are tied to us with bonds of love that can't be broken.

In racially and/or culturally diverse parishes, it's best to have team members from the various groups. Having separate programs for each group seems to be a waste of resources and is more divisive than unifying. There are many types of exclusivity within our faith communities that must be addressed and rectified. All methods of screening out and marginalizing must be confronted and eliminated if we are to truly follow Jesus' example of welcoming all. Each parish has its own unique challenges. Whether it concerns social class, income, race, sexual orientation, religion or the lack of religion, all types of exclusivity must be challenged and replaced with welcoming outreach. Keep in mind that if your parish extends an invitation to all, you must be ready and willing for "all" to accept that invitation.

Most returnees are very wounded and skittish about coming back to the Church. Those who return are of all ages and come from very different backgrounds. Like the emergency room of a hospital, anyone can walk in the door. The concept of any program for returning Catholics is to welcome everyone, *no matter what level they are at* and to make sure that activities and content are geared toward those who are the most needy. The content and structure is designed to welcome back the most fragile and skeptical because the others who are more confident or assured will also be comfortable if the most needy are cared for. It's possible that unbaptized and/or unconfirmed people will attend the Catholics Returning Home sessions and they may eventually continue in the RCIA to become Catholic. I think it's best to let them proceed at their own pace as they're ready. If we attempt to screen people attending a returning-Catholics program, we may discourage them from connecting with the Church. It may benefit these people to get comfortable with the Church through this type of program and then, later on, they may have the confidence to continue toward becoming Catholic through the RCIA process.

As noted earlier, most of the returnees are at a grade-school level in their understanding of Catholicism. They may be highly educated and successful in their lives and careers, but they are usually at stage one concerning Catholicism. This is not to say they don't have faith or belief in God. Many are prayerful and have a very strong and positive faith life. Most have a good relationship with God, but may have a negative opinion of the Church. Many have tried all sorts of other

religions, especially Protestant Christian churches. In fact, many return because they become offended when some representatives of
the Protestant church they are attending starts criticizing the Catholic Church. For many of these returning Catholics, those criticisms
by the Protestant church toward Catholicism awaken their faith in
and love for the Catholic Church. This is why when people ask me
what to do if their friends or relatives or acquaintances start attending Protestant churches, I tell them it's good they went to a Protestant church because that may be the quickest way to reawaken their
faith and love for the Catholic Church. When the Protestant church
starts to go against the grain of a Catholicism so deeply rooted, many
ricochet back to the Faith.

Getting the Word Out

The key to a ministry to inactive Catholics is publicity because there
is a huge group of disconnected Catholics out there. The Roman
Catholic denomination is the largest in the United States (sixty million). What is the second largest denomination in the United States?
The answer: nonpracticing Catholics. There are approximately
twenty million inactive Catholics in the United States. As stated
earlier, some Protestant churches target and recruit these inactive
Catholics. In any given Catholic parish, approximately fifty percent
of the registered parishioners do not attend Mass on any regular,
weekly basis. Besides those on the parish rosters, there are innumer-
able inactive Catholics adrift who are not connected to any parish.
The publicity used in a Catholics Returning Home program can be
an outdoor sign or marquee, articles in the parish bulletin, church
announcements by the lector and the presider, free notices in the
religion section of the newspaper, full-page flyers stuffed into bulletins, flyers posted on the doors of local businesses, brochures, announcements in regular parish mailings, notices sent to the parents of children attending the parish school as well as the parents
of Parish School of Religion (PSR) students, intentions included

in the prayers of the faithful, and television and radio spots. (See Chapter 7, "Publicity.")

In spreading the word, no publicity is wasted. Perhaps just by seeing the invitation through the publicity, people will return to the Church even if they don't attend any of the program sessions. Many will just start attending Mass again and others will bring their children to be baptized or register them to attend PSR or the school proper.

Most inactive Catholics are open to an invitation to return to the Church if it's done in a kind, compassionate, nonjudgmental manner. Nagging, chasing, and hounding an inactive Catholic will not work to bring someone back. In fact, it will drive them away all the more. Accusing someone of abandoning the faith or of being immoral or evil will never work. Recently I got a call from the pastor of a parish asking for more information about the Catholics Returning Home program. He had seen a newspaper article about the program. I gave him an overview and explained briefly that it was a ministry of compassion. Then I began to talk about why people leave the Church. At this point the pastor interrupted me and very forcefully said in a matter-of-fact manner that "the reason people leave the Church is because they're lazy, immoral, and focused on materialism and consumerism." He went on to say that the number of attendees in his parish's returning-Catholics program has been going down for some time. Would you want to come back to this parish? Chastising someone for not contributing to the Church will not work. Our treasure frequently follows our hearts. Thus, if someone isn't paying money to the Church, it's because their heart isn't with the Church. If their hearts are touched, their minds, bodies, souls, and even pocketbooks will follow. Catholics Returning Home must never be built on asking the returnees back for their contributions. However, if they are invited back and treated compassionately and kindly, many are so touched that they generously give of themselves including their time, treasure, and talent. Many returnees come back and become very involved in the ministry of Catholics Returning Home as well as other ministries in the parish.

The concept of returning home is very descriptive and seems to capture the heart and essence of the ministry. It seems to touch the hearts of those who have left and call out to them. Those who have left recognize immediately its appeal as a calling out to them in a caring, personal manner. For example, when we put up outdoor signs or an announcement on the parish marquee that Catholics Returning Home will be beginning soon, we get numerous calls from nonpracticing Catholics who immediately recognize what the ministry entails based on name recognition alone. It doesn't matter that they've been away from the Church for many years, they still recognize that the Catholic Church is inviting them to return. The name recognition is very important because as people are living very pressured and busy lives, those who are away from the Church may see our publicity and signs for only a moment. Since we're grabbing their attention briefly, it's critical that we make a lasting impression in that short amount of time. The name "Catholics Returning Home" accomplishes that objective. Therefore, the name of the program and its essential structure should be left intact for best results.

Format and Structure

I suggest that parishes offer a returning-Catholics program three times per year: the Christmas season, the Easter season, and the Fall. "Come Home for Christmas," "Come Home for Easter," and "Come Home in the Fall"—the same six-week series is repeated each time. It is a small-group, faith-sharing process similar to RCIA in that storytelling and bonding serve as the foundation rather than a lecture-based format. The series is offered after Christmas, after Easter, and in September (near the beginning of the new school year). The publicity and outreach efforts begin six weeks before Christmas and Easter and throughout August if the Fall series starts in mid-September. Programs are offered at those specific times of the year because that's when the call to return to the Church is most strongly felt by nonpracticing Catholics. It takes a tremendous amount of effort to come back to the Church after being away for many years. However, nonpracticing Catholics seem to be open to the spirit of the season at Christmas and Easter. In the Fall, people seem to have a need to reconnect with the Church because their children are returning to PSR or the parish school and the outreach efforts of the RCIA process move these people to reflect on their Catholicism.

For some small and/or rural parishes where the Catholic population is small, offering the program once or twice per year is an option. The largest number of returnees come back at Christmas, the next largest is at Easter, and the smallest number is in the Fall. The number of attendees is linked directly to how well the publicity gets out. The largest group I've experienced has been about thirty-five. Usually, the numbers vary from five to fifteen. An ideal size is no more then fifteen. With larger groups over fifteen, it's difficult to attend to each of the returnees on a personal basis. They're very fragile and need a lot of personalized, individual attention and mentoring.

I recommend conducting a returning-Catholics program in a "managed or structured" support-group format that includes topical updates covering the basics of Catholicism. The first two weeks of the six-week series are structured in a storytelling, faith-sharing, "managed support group" format. Those sessions in weeks three through five consist of topical updates on the basics of Catholicism involving the Church today, the Mass, and an explanation of the sacrament of penance (confession). The sixth and final session consists of both a topical update, a discussion of the Nicene Creed, and a wrap-up of the series that includes the completion of an evaluation form by the attendees as well as an invitation for them to participate as members of upcoming returning-Catholics ministry teams.

The first two sessions are the most important of the series. The last session is also very important as it assures returnees of being part of a continuing, lifelong faith journey within the Church. The three topical update sessions are important in the sense of bringing those returning "up to speed" on the basics of Catholicism and to feel comfortable within the Church. The first two sessions are important because they allow the returnees to share their stories in a managed, structured format. Most of the returnees are rather calm, collected, easygoing, and just glad to be back in the parish church. However, all it takes is one or two people to disrupt and monopolize the group. Since anyone can show up, it's impossible to know who will be attending. Some returnees could be there to quote Scripture from a fundamentalist perspective and argue with everyone. Others are disruptive for a variety of reasons and they will try to bring up every controversial issue just to argue.

By following the suggested agenda for the first and second sessions, the team leaders can "manage" the group such that if one or more of the attendees gets disruptive and out of line, the team leader can easily but firmly return the discussion back to the agenda item and avert an argument. Although the agenda should be followed closely, it's ideal if the flow of the evening is done to look seamless. In other words, it's best if the evening is managed and conducted by the team leader without referring to an actual agenda. The returnees are more comfortable and open up more if the evening is "managed" and flows—seemingly naturally—rather than looking rigid or controlled. The six-week series is designed to invite people back, make them feel welcome, allow them the opportunity to vent their comments and concerns in a safe manner, become updated about the basics of Catholicism, and aid them in reconnecting to a parish and becoming active members.

Continued Faith Development

It's important to have ongoing adult education and small-group faith-sharing ministries within a parish in order to route returnees in their continued faith development. Many returnees want to continue the series beyond the six weeks. This is a wonderful affirmation of just how well a Catholics Returning Home program can "work"—to bring someone back into the fold who felt totally separated from the Church, and in the space of six weeks to have that person experience such a transformation that they want to continue their development within the Church—this is truly the work of the Spirit. However, I recommend that additional sessions be presented separately in the Spring and Fall and opened up to the entire parish. It's good for returnees to mix with other parishioners and become fully incorporated into parish life; it also makes sense to invite the entire parish to such continuing formation classes in order to take full advantage of such varied resources and efforts. One such continuing education topic should delve into annulments/divorce and remarriage. Some parishes regularly offer an annulment series once per year in the Spring or Fall. If a group of parishes work together to present a returning-Catholics program, it's convenient to have one parish specialize in putting on the series for the returnees and others present the ongoing adult education/formation such as presenting an annual seminar on annulments.

CHAPTER 3

Basic Program Requirements for Catholics Returning Home

~

Catholics Returning Home and the RCIA

The Catholics Returning Home program has evolved over the years. Initially, I offered the six-week program twice per year after Christmas beginning in January and after Easter beginning the week after Easter with the outreach publicity done during Advent and Lent. I also expanded the program to offer it starting in mid-September because many PSR and school parents want to reconnect with the Church when they register their children. In addition, the RCIA outreach seemed to bring forth a number of former Catholics and there was no place for them since RCIA is for those initially becoming Catholic. Some parishes put returning Catholics into the RCIA group without having a separate program for returning Catholics. The two don't mix well together.

Most returning Catholics have some degree of anger and hostility toward the Church whereas the people becoming Catholic are coming in with minimal prior experience of the Catholic Church. Returning Catholics in an RCIA group tend to feel out of place because they're not included in any of the RCIA ceremonies and rituals. Many say they feel almost jealous that newcomers are given all this attention and special treatment while they are excluded and can only observe as onlookers. They say they feel like second-class citizens or displaced foster children who are brought in through the back door. The answer is not to design a special ritual for returning Catholics because most do not want to be put on public display. Most returning Catholics prefer to remain private so they can proceed at their own pace, in their own way. Another reason to keep returning Catholics separate from the RCIA is because those becoming Catholic get impatient and frustrated with some of the returning Catholic's negative emotions.

In small parishes, the RCIA group and the returning-Catholics groups can be combined for the third through fifth weeks as regards the updates on the Church today, explanation of the Mass, and an explanation of the sacrament of penance. But this consolidation must be handled carefully. Many returnees are very aware of slight, skittish and uncertain about their status in the Church; they are particularly sensitive to being "shuffled around" and mixed with another group of strangers. During the group process and sharing of the first two weeks of the program, the returnees and the team bond to form a small, close-knit faith community anchored by trust, so it's risky to disrupt and change those dynamics in midstream. For returning Catholics, the team is their link or tie with the Church. Many form lifelong bonds with the team members. The small-group faith community *is* "church" to the returning Catholics. It is the place where they are accepted, welcomed, listened to without being judged. The atmosphere of the small group should be nonjudgmental acceptance. For those Catholics Returning Home groups that I've led personally, I've found the best approach is to keep the RCIA groups and the returning Catholics completely separate.

A Welcoming Space Is Necessary

During the early to mid 1980s, as I was discerning my call from the Lord, I got involved in a variety of ministries, from nursing home visitation to being a team member of an RCIA program for a group of parishes who were working in tandem. My husband and I were the team leaders for our parish. Our responsibility was to conduct the outreach publicity for our parish and take the initial phone calls from prospective candidates and then route them to the combined RCIA gatherings. One summer, as we were blitzing our parish with bulletin announcements, flyers, and notices on the marquee, we also attended the Sunday morning after-Mass, coffee-and-donut social in order to meet with prospective RCIA candidates in a social setting. One elderly lady came up to us, in tears, and begged us to help her with her children. She said she had been away from the Church for many years after she got a divorce. Just as painful for this woman was the fact that her seven children were not attending church. Her older children were baptized and some had completed the sacraments of initiation, but the younger ones weren't even baptized because as she fell away from the Church, her family lost touch with the ministers and the parish community. She begged us to talk with her children and invite them back to the Church because she was sure they would listen to us rather than her. She gave me the names and phone numbers of those who lived in the area and I called and talked with them. Initially, they were quite hesitant, but I assured them they were welcome to come back to the Church and they could attend the RCIA initial inquiry session with no strings attached.

After the initial RCIA inquiry meeting, I got another call from this poor lady, again in tears. She said of all her children that we invited to return, only one had the courage to try coming back. This lady had encouraged all of her children to attend the initial RCIA inquiry session because she thought it was a welcoming group for all coming back to the Church. The daughter that came to the RCIA inquiry session had already been baptized and had received her first Communion but hadn't been confirmed. So, when she went to the inquiry session, the Sister who was the director of the multi-parish RCIA group met her at the door and "interviewed" her about her prior sacramental preparation. When the daughter said she had already received all of the sacraments of initiation except confirmation, the sister told her in a matter-of-fact manner that she didn't belong there because she was already Catholic. This young woman was crushed and went home in tears. She hadn't had any connection with the Church for a number of years, following the disintegration of a marriage that ended in divorce. Subsequently she felt so ashamed of this "failure" that she couldn't bring herself to attend church. Then, after finally getting her courage up to try coming back to the parish, this Sister told her she didn't belong there, and the young woman was totally and completely devastated and alienated. I tried to assure her that a huge mistake was made and Sister really didn't mean she wasn't welcome to return to the Church—that Sister had meant the RCIA group was for non-Catholics interested in converting—but I doubt my message got through after this religious Sister told her just the opposite. I was furious and wrote a letter to the chancery and asked where former Catholics should be routed within the Catholic Church to reintegrate them since they didn't "belong" in the RCIA. If the Catholic Church doesn't want former Catholics, the local Protestant churches are more than happy to take them. Soon after this episode, I established a returning Catholics program in another church in the area.

If we look to the parable of the Prodigal Son (Lk 15:11–32), the returning son was welcomed, fully restored to his position as son, and his family threw a party for him and had a huge celebration. Again, in the parable of the Lost Sheep (Lk 15:4–7), Jesus the Good Shepherd speaks of leaving the ninety-nine and searching out the one who has strayed, and bringing it back to the fold. The angels of heaven rejoiced over the return of the one who had strayed. As disciples, shouldn't we try to model these parables when we're welcoming returning Catholics? Returning Catholics need to be made to feel welcome by the Church, made to feel that they're missed, that they're special, and that they belong. They need to know they have a "place" in the Church. They should have their own group where they can safely vent and share their stories. They need to be listened to without being judged as being unforgivable sinners because, in my experience, most are more sinned against than sinners themselves.

Be Prepared to Listen to and Share Stories of Deep Hurt

Most people who have left the Church have a "church story" within which lies a big bundle of hurts. They may cite a reason for leaving which isn't the real or "root" cause. For example, some will say they have disagreements with some of the Church's theological positions, but after further discussion, they'll say they tried to arrange a wedding or funeral and the parish staff was unfriendly or uncooperative. Whatever the real reason for their leaving the Church, perception is reality. It doesn't matter whether their reason is real or imagined, it's their reality. Sometimes the reasons cited are really awful, and one immediately thinks it's no wonder that this person got mad and left. Other times, after listening to the reason for leaving, one wonders if that's all there is to it. How could anyone take offense at such an inconsequential event! Fr. McKee said that one person told him he left the Church because "Father" never shook his hand after Mass, whereas "Father" shook hands with everybody else. Most likely that person had other things going on in his life that made him so sensitive to slight, but there is no way of knowing for sure.

During the first two sessions of the returning Catholics program, the team and returnees share their stories of leaving and returning. This allows the team and returnees to bond and the returnees to feel affirmed, accepted, and comfortable in a new environment. It helps to have "witness talks" by Catholics who have been away and returned, though it is also a good idea to have Catholics who have never left share their struggles as well as their reasons for staying. This helps returnees feel more comfortable about returning to the Church.

For the sake of continuity and stability, it's best to have one team in place for the entire six-week series so the returnees can develop trust and feel comfortable with them. Some of the returnees and team members develop lifelong friendships. Some parishes have attempted to have a different team each week; this can be very confusing and unsettling to the returnees and most likely will result in a high dropout rate. Many returnees come back each week because of the bonds of friendship they have formed with team members.

Throughout the six weeks of the Catholics Returning Home series, it's important to stress that the Church is made up of imperfect human beings who make mistakes. As Fr. Mckee says, the Church isn't made up of angels. Thus, it's important for returnees to know that they will never find perfection within the Church, simply a faith community of flawed human beings. It's also important to share information about the various ministries within the Church and to stress that the initial six weeks are just the beginning of their journey. Some returnees attend the series several times because they want to hear everything again. It's good to have various small-group ministries to route returnees to after they have completed the series. A Catholics Returning Home program works best at parishes that are reasonably active and friendly, with a variety of ministries to offer returnees. The faith community should be open to welcoming new members.

The Support of the Parish Is Essential

A returning-Catholics program should be lay-driven, like-to-like, grass-roots ministry. While the priests and support staff do not have to have hands-on, day-to-day involvement in the program, they should be supportive. Although our pastor is very supportive of our Catholics Returning Home program, he has minimal involvement in the planning and administration of the program. I try to schedule all our priests and deacons for specific segments of the program so that participants have a chance to meet the various ordained ministers. I usually have our pastor and/or deacons conduct the segment on "The Church Today: Changes Since Vatican II," the Mass, and the sacrament of penance.

It's important to work with the resources that you have in a particular parish. If there are fewer priests and deacons and instead more lay staff, then include them in the update portions of the program. Catholics Returning Home works with whatever resources you have.

Some parishes that have a larger number of priests end up utilizing more priests for the updates while other parishes utilize lay staff or deacons because that's what they have available to them. In my experience, the most important quality for the presenters to have is an attitude of compassion and acceptance and the ability to communicate and relate to returnees at their level.

When You're Leading the Ministry

The Catholics Returning Home ministry should be led by a team of at least two people who are compassionate, good listeners, and sensitive to the needs of those who have been away from the Church. It is not necessary that team members be "mini-theologians." However, they should be nonjudgmental in their approach to returnees. Some types of people who don't fit in well on the team are those with strict, legal, rigoristic viewpoints. It's best to handpick prospective team members rather than selecting people with the necessary skills by putting a notice in the bulletin. It's good to have some team members who have been away from the Church and returned. It's not necessary to have returnees on the initial team because you will recruit team members from each group as they return.

When I first began this ministry, I asked the attendees if they wanted to be on my team as I conducted future series. Although it may seem to border on the ridiculous to ask someone to help with the next outreach when they themselves have recently returned, it's actually very beneficial to all concerned. Helping others return to the Church is very healing for those recently returned. It is also very inspirational for newcomers to see others who have been back only a short time already bursting with enthusiasm and zeal to share the good news. Returnees find it very affirming to be trusted enough to be on the team, and they are frequently the most dynamic and enthusiastic members. Of course they shouldn't be given team responsibilities that are beyond their abilities, but at a minimum they could share their stories and help with some of the footwork.

Dealing With Angry and Hostile Returnees

When I began the Catholics Returning Home program, the sessions were structured primarily as a support group. Over time I learned that without a managed structure, the group tended to get bogged down with trivial and controversial issues. It was very counterproductive to allow the returnees to ask open-ended questions since all it took was a couple angry people to wrest away control of the group and mire the proceedings into a litany of controversial questions that couldn't be answered. Once the group gets negative, it's very hard to regain control. Instead of being productive and healing, the group gets stuck in controversy and hostility. The few angry and hostile members dominate the group and everyone else is held captive. Thus, I developed a syllabus of topics that covers the basics of Catholicism and a weekly agenda to be used as a management tool to control the meeting. Following the agenda is crucial for the first two weeks in order to ensure that the group stays on track and the attendees acquire updated information without drifting off onto tangents that can't be resolved.

Apart from some brief introductory remarks at the first session, priests shouldn't come to the first two sessions so that the group can speak more freely about the difficulties they faced with the Church. For some angry or frightened folks, a priest makes them even more angry or afraid to speak out. Our pastor or associate comes in the first night for ten minutes to welcome them back to the Church and apologize for any hurts that the Church may have caused them. It's important that the welcoming priest is genuine and friendly. I tell the visiting priest to "show a lot of teeth" (smile) and leave. It is safer to exclude the priest from the first two sessions; otherwise it's very easy for some of the angrier returnees to focus on "the priest" and make him the brunt of all of their displaced anger, hostility, and rage. This is unhealthy and unproductive for all concerned, especially the poor priest.

In the early years of conducting the Catholics Returning Home program, as I was learning through trial and error, a visiting priest decided to attend our group of returning Catholics. He was particularly enthusiastic and excited about evangelization because he had just completed some special training on discipleship and evangelization and even had personal "business" cards that included his name and title as "Evangelist." This episode I am going to relay to you occurred during the first couple of evenings of the series where the sharing and storytelling take place. There were two extremely angry and hostile people in the group. One had recently gone through a very lengthy and bitter divorce. The other's spouse had recently died. Both were intensely angry at God, the world, the Church, and everybody else as they struggled with their losses. Well, in walks this bright-eyed and bushy-tailed priest. He was smiling ear to ear, and told them how excited and happy he was to be there with them as he handed out his business cards. Instantaneously, those two returnees verbally pounced on him with every bit of pent-up spite, anger, and hostility they had built up over the years. They barely let him get a word out of his mouth. They attacked him and blamed him for every negative thing that had ever happened in the Catholic Church. They verbally eviscerated him! At times, he looked like he was about to burst into tears and the two angry attackers seemed to enjoy his misery. Because I didn't have a working agenda, it was impossible for me to regain control of the meeting without alienating everybody in the group. All of us were held hostage for the remainder of the meeting. It's no surprise that this particular priest never came back to my sessions after that evening! I learned to carefully select or exclude priests from the first two sessions and to have a "tight" agenda so as to manage and control the content.

I've designed Catholics Returning Home to include the principles of "tough love" from the support-group programs I've attended. This means that we welcome returnees and accept them with compassion, kindness, and love. However, we will maintain sufficient structure and boundaries within the group through the use of an agenda or syllabus so that everyone is treated with dignity and respect, especially members of the team, priests, deacons, and lay presenters. By utilizing the anonymous questionnaire (see page 58), returnees can share on paper instead of unloading on others. Venting and sharing is managed by following the agenda so that the group doesn't end up in a barefisted brawl. Managing the group in an effort to keep the mood positive is healing and uplifting for all concerned, because if the group ends up being a total complaint session, nobody will want to come back—including the team members.

During implementation of a Catholics Returning Home program, some parishes have expanded my suggested questionnaire in order to allow returnees to ask everything they ever wanted to know about the Catholic Church. One parish even eliminated the anonymous questionnaire and instead replaced it with a "blank" piece of paper to give the returnees the freedom to ask whatever they want. This is a big mistake, a really huge blunder! To make such a change will more than likely end up in disaster. The reason being is that the anonymous questionnaire is a psychological tool designed to lead returnees down a path to healing and growth. It allows them to vent in a safe, structured manner without harming others.

After hearing about the purpose of the anonymous questionnaire, one of Fr. McKee's Redemptorist confreres said to me: "You have to throw up before you feel better." He is absolutely correct. The anonymous questionnaire allows returnees to "throw up" on paper instead of on the team. When people are angry and confused, it's better for them to vent that pent-up, displaced anger and hostility onto an anonymous questionnaire instead of directing it at others. To give an angry, confused, and hostile group of returnees a blank piece of paper or an open forum to ask whatever they want is an invitation to disaster. They will steer the topics toward every controversial issue in the Church. Even if most of the returnees are relatively even-tempered and calm, all it takes is one or more angry souls in the group to wrest control and dominate the discussion, and it's almost impossible to take control back without alienating everyone in the group. Moral of the story: stick with the agenda and syllabus in order to maintain control of the group; otherwise, the group will become hostile and unproductive rather than healing and uplifting. The goal of the Catholics Returning Home sessions is to provide a safe haven for returnees where they can have a positive experience of the Church in a small-group setting. Individual team members can answer returnees' specific—and perhaps tangential—questions by staying after the sessions and talking with them or by calling them by phone.

Additional Resources May Be Necessary

When I started the Catholics Returning Home program many years ago, ministry to nonpracticing Catholics wasn't very popular. Thus, I didn't get much support from parishes. So, in order to conduct the ministry, I acquired a number of videos on the recurrent topics which I would use at the meetings if speakers weren't available. The topics cover the basics of Catholicism, such as the Mass, the sacrament of penance, the Second Vatican Council, the Nicene Creed, the seven sacraments, Mary and the saints, prayer and spirituality, and forming a Christian conscience. I found videos to be very useful because they allowed me to borrow from the "experts" whenever I wanted. This way, I didn't need to know everything. Whenever I showed a video, I also had an open discussion afterward so the attendees could assimilate the information. It's best to have live speakers for the update evenings because it allows the returnees to relate and interact with members of the ministerial staff, but if these people are not available the videos will suffice. It's important to work with whatever you have at a particular parish.

Sponsoring a returning-Catholics program is a very economical ministry. Most of the publicity can be accomplished by using outside signs, flyers, bulletin articles, news releases for newspapers, cable TV and radio spots, and announcements during or after Mass by both the presider and lay lector. Newspaper ads can be used, but are relatively expensive. When I conduct my program, I make available inexpensive catechisms for participants to purchase. The "Stories of Faith From Catholics Returning Home" and the other optional videos are relatively inexpensive. (See Appendix, pages 101–104 for a listing of books and videos.) The outdoor signs are also fairly inexpensive and can be reused indefinitely.

CHAPTER 4

Checklist for Starting a Catholics Returning Home Program

~

For some folks who are highly involved in parish ministry, some of the steps I've included on this checklist might seem obvious. However, a Catholics Returning Home program seems to attract many who are new to working in ministry within the Catholic Church. Therefore, they don't know the ropes and are unsure of where to start. The steps below are based on actual questions people have asked me over the years.

1. **Make sure the pastor and parish administrative structure have approved of and fully support a Catholics Returning Home program.**

    Each parish has a different administrative structure. Usually, the pastor is in charge and there are various paid and volunteer employees with various councils and committees carrying out specific tasks and ministries. The first step in getting a Catholics Returning Home program started in your parish is to talk with the pastor; he will direct you to the right staff person and/or committee that would be responsible for the Catholics Returning Home program. It is paramount that the pastor and the respective staff person or committee has approved of and supports these efforts. In many parishes, you will need to meet with the

39

respective committee and even the parish council to explain what the program entails, why it is needed, and how it relates to the parish's overall goals and objectives. You will also need to provide an estimate of the cost of implementing and running the program. This cost is minimal and primarily depends on the decision to invest in outdoor signs, videos, flyers, and brochures. Since the pope, NCCB (National Conference of Catholic Bishops), and most arch/dioceses now rate reaching out to inactive Catholics as one of their top priorities, many parishes are interested in implementing this ministry. However, sometimes it can take months or even years to get a parish interested in a specific program that makes reaching out to inactive Catholics its primary focus. It helps that the Catholics Returning Home program is widely used and accepted, and approved by the NCCB.

Once the pastor and parish administrative structure have approved the program, they need to understand the time line for implementation and what their initial and ongoing responsibilities are going to be. They need to commit to providing the necessary budget, human resources, and support for the program. They also need to "buy into" helping spread the word for inviting people back, welcoming them, and being prepared to accept them back into the parish. The pastor and the administrative structure can work wonders in gaining support from the rest of the parish by setting the proper welcoming environment. The pastor can do everything or nothing for this program. If he's not behind it, it will go nowhere. He doesn't have to have much "hands on," day-to-day involvement for the program to succeed, but if he is vocal in his support of the program and the people who serve it, Catholics Returning Home can blossom in that parish.

2. Team selection and formation

The team should have a minimum of two to five members and one person should be in charge. If the community is racially or culturally diverse, the team should have representatives from the different groups. Avoid selecting those who are overcommitted and on every church committee. Catholics Returning Home needs team members who have a calling specific to this ministry and the time and commitment to devote it. This program is an "up close and personal" ministry. Frequently, team members form lifelong bonds and friendships with returnees. Team members should be willing to have that kind of closeness or intimacy with returnees.

It's not necessary that team members have "heavy duty" theological backgrounds. However, they should be comfortable with their own faith. The most important trait of team members is the ability to accept returnees where they're at without judging them or wanting to fix them or remake them in their own image. This usually takes someone who is relatively comfortable with themselves and their own faith journey. Personality types to avoid are those who are rigid, black-and-white legalistic types who want to "save those big sinners." As noted earlier, it's great to have a mixture of those who have been away and returned to the Church as well as those who have never left.

Make sure all the team members have read the first three chapters of this book for background information on the dynamics of the "managed support group" process. This helps team members realize that they're not supposed to chase down and "fix" returnees or that they have to know everything and have answers to every question or detail that comes up, especially within the actual sessions. During the first two sessions, the team needs to understand their role in keeping the group on track and not going off onto tangents and opening up controversial issues. It's important for the team members to be willing to open up and share some of their own personal stories. They need to be able to do this naturally, without making it look forced or contrived—this helps returnees feel more comfortable.

The team should work on developing their listening skills. Listening means being present, paying attention to and accepting someone else's comments. Returning Catholics are very confused and have minimal understanding of the Catholic faith. Thus, sometimes, they voice some rather strange, uninformed thoughts and opinions about Catholicism. Don't argue with them at this point; just allow them to say what they feel. Even if you were to win such an argument, you would risk losing any number of returnees and turning them off to the Church. Sometimes, they may purposely say ridiculous and controversial things just to mask their insecurity or lack of knowledge of the Catholic faith. Try to find something to agree with in whatever they said, or tell them that's interesting or that it's another point of view. Usually if you accept them and agree with them—at least on some point of common ground—they're satisfied. During the sessions, stick to the agenda items and try not to bring in any other topics or issues so as to avoid "opening up a can of worms." Team members can talk with the returnees individually after the sessions or in a phone conversation to discuss their personal situations and answer open-ended questions.

3.   Room reservations and program schedule

Every parish has different methods of scheduling the meeting rooms. Our parish has a year-long master calendar room schedule which opens up each June. Thus, we schedule all the meeting rooms for the next year in June for June through May of the next year. Of course, in order to schedule the rooms, one must already have the yearly schedule for the Catholics Returning Home program. We schedule the three series as follows: the after-Christmas series starts the first week of January; the after-Easter series starts the first week after Easter; and the fall series starts in mid-September.

Try to get rooms that are comfortable and easy to access. For example, a large gym is less conducive to small-group sharing than a small room with comfortable chairs. If the room is located in the basement at the end of a winding hallway which is hard to find, many returnees are likely to get lost and not find the room. The best location is in a meeting room in or near the church so that the group can gather around the altar and say the Our Father at the close of each session. However, you must do the best you can with whatever it is you have available.

4. **Presenter schedule for the next year**

In June, when we schedule the meeting rooms for the next year, I send a program schedule to our pastor. He confirms his schedule to make sure he's available. He also schedules the various deacons for specific sessions. In addition, before each series begins, I send another copy of the six-week schedule to the priests and deacons to remind them of when they're to attend and what they should be prepared to do. The presenters also need to have a copy of the outline or summary of the session so they know what it is they're supposed to talk about for their specific session. For example, send a copy of the session outline or summary to the presenters for that evening and let them preview the video for Session 3, page 66. The presenters need guidance—we can't assume they just "know" what to talk about. In addition, I send the presenters copies of the summary of the anonymous questionnaires so they have a better sense of the "personality" of this specific group.

5. **Publicity and timing**

The publicity for a Catholics Returning Home series should begin six weeks before sessions start up and continue until the week prior to the series' first-week session. For the Christmas series, the publicity should begin after Thanksgiving; for the Easter series, publicity kicks off at the beginning of Lent; and for the Fall series, publicity starts near the end of July. The publicity should include bulletin articles, an outdoor sign, free newspaper news releases (if possible), flyers, brochures, prayers of the faithful, and announcements after and during Christmas and Easter

Masses and a couple of weeks before the beginning of the Fall series. If the parish has a Web site, a page devoted to Catholics Returning Home should be included along with a contact name, e-mail address, and/or phone number. For example, St. Rita's Parish in Rockford, Illinois, has a very distinctive and effective Web page (http://www.stritarockford.org) for their Catholics Returning Home program that includes music.

It's important to stop the outreach publicity when the new series begins or else you'll continue to get new people coming throughout the series. It's best that new people start at the beginning and attend both the first and second session because that's where the storytelling, venting, and sharing occurs. However, if people get the courage to come forward and ask to attend, I don't like to make then wait for months until the next series starts. Therefore, I'm up front with them, and I make it clear to them that they are at a disadvantage by not starting at the beginning but that they are most welcome to join the group. Even though they come in after the first session, I still have them complete the anonymous questionnaire (see page 58) to allow them to "catch up" with the rest of the group by expressing their feelings. Although the outreach publicity should be discontinued when the new series starts, you should put articles in the bulletin that inform the congregation of the results of the series. Through bulletin announcements, I inform parishioners how many people attended the series. It's important to provide the congregation with feedback so they will continue their involvement and participation in outreach efforts and in welcoming returnees into the community.

Most parishes have unique requirements and schedules for placing articles in their bulletins. Before every six-week series, I update all the bulletin articles with the current dates and note within each article the week each article should be published. Then I give both a hard copy and diskette to our bulletin editor so she has everything in a timely manner.

Our parish has separate people who schedule the prayers of

the faithful and the parish announcements. Therefore, I prepare a schedule listing exactly what I want them to do with the corresponding dates and I give them copies well ahead of time.

If you are expanding your media outlets to newspapers and cable television stations, you will have to obtain the addresses for these. Some have their own unique forms that you must complete. I send out the news releases a couple of times because most newspapers publish them only once. In our parish, we include one-page bulletin inserts with the upcoming year's schedule of Catholics Returning Home; this means we have to meet the publication deadline. If people attend Mass only once or twice a year, it's important to get a long-range schedule into their hands so they can plan accordingly.

The outdoor sign is really critical. I prefer to use simple wording such as: "Catholics Returning Home program begins soon, call St. Pat's at xxx-xxxx." I have my phone number all over the place, on signs, newspapers, and flyers, and I've never received a crank phone call. If you don't want to put someone's phone number on the sign, you can use the parish number. But if you do this, you must make sure that people are prepared to take the calls. At our parish, we have volunteer teenagers taking the phone calls. (These teens have a lot of unfocused enthusiasm and energy.) When they take a call, they record the names and phone numbers of returnees and pass that information on to the team members. In addition, they also give the team members' names and phone numbers to the callers. When the team members take the initial calls, it's important that they're friendly, accepting, and that they make the effort to find out how the returnee found out about the series. After you get the person's name and phone number, explain to them the basics of the program and that they're very welcome to attend.

At Christmas and Easter Masses, all the priests should say a few words of welcome to returning Catholics and invite them to the upcoming sessions. It's magic if it comes out of the priests' mouths. Many returnees have said they just happened to attend

Mass at Christmas or Easter after being away for many years, and Father welcomed back the returning Catholics, and they just knew it was meant for them. It's critical that the priests are given a write-up of what they're supposed to talk about and when. Some people have said, "Father should know how to do this without me telling him." Not true. Father doesn't know he's supposed to do these things. We need to help Father by letting him know beforehand what we'd like him to do.

CHAPTER 5

Details of Six-Week Sessions

∽

SESSION #1

Welcome/Completion of Anonymous Questionnaires

Items to have on hand and things to do before the session starts:

- Two to five team members wearing name tags identifying them as team members
- A comfortable, easy-to-find meeting room with table and chairs
- Signs and greeters outside directing people how to find the meeting room
- A candle and lighter
- A box of tissues
- Name tags for team and attendees
- Pens/pencils for attendees
- A listing of team members, including phone numbers
- Copies of the Prayer of Thomas Merton
- Schedule for Catholics Returning Home six-week series showing topics by week
- Blank, initial anonymous questionnaires
- Sign-in Sheet
- Copies of *Handbook for Today's Catholic* (I recommend this

book because it is simple and easy-to-understand) by Liguori Publications to be available for returnees (available from Liguori, see page 106)

- Copies of recent parish bulletins and any other information about parish activities
- Copies of *Returning Home to Your Catholic Faith* by Sally Mews, published by Liguori (2003). I recommend this book for returnees, because it is a compassionate invitation and guide for their return to the Church which parallels the sessions (see page 106).
- Optional: Invite the pastor or associate to stop by and introduce himself and welcome them back to the Church. It helps if the priest makes a "genuine" apology for any hurts they've experienced from the Church. If the priest isn't comfortable making an apology, it's best not to attempt this if it's not done in a genuine manner.
- Optional: Prerecorded background music and/or beverages and snacks
- Optional: Invite leaders from the divorced/remarriage and bereavement ministries to attend the meeting and introduce themselves to the returnees.
- Optional video: "An Invitation, With No Strings Attached" (Liguori, see page 101)

The Holy Spirit is the inspiration and guide for any returning-Catholics program. Anyone called to this ministry either as a team leader or as a returnee is called by the Holy Spirit. By including petitions for returning Catholics in the Mass, we're asking for the grace of the Holy Spirit. Throughout the preparation for meetings and in the meetings themselves, all the team members should pray for the Spirit's guidance and help. In addition, many parishes ask any surrounding religious communities and monasteries for prayer before and throughout the series. Some Catholics Returning Home teams meet fifteen minutes before the sessions and pray to the Holy Spirit for guidance throughout the evening.

The first session is the most important of the six sessions, because it sets the tone for the rest of the series. If people get the nerve up to come to the first session and have a good experience, they will most likely continue.

Priests shouldn't attend the first or second sessions in whole because some returnees are afraid of priests and some get angrier when priests are there. If our pastor or associate is available, they stop in for ten minutes to greet the returnees, smile, and apologize to them for any hurts the Church has caused them.

The room should be easy to find and comfortable. It's better to have a smaller, cozier room than a big open gym or parish hall. There should be outdoor and indoor signs pointing out how to find the meeting room. Greeters should be outside telling people where the room is and helping them as needed. I like to have a candle burning on the table. The team members should have name tags identifying them as part of the team. I prefer having a table with chairs around it instead of just chairs because the group will be writing.

I have the meeting run from 7:30–9:00 P.M. For the first session, I start about ten minutes late to allow late arrivers time to get there. I do make it a point to end on time at 9:00 P.M., telling the attendees that we stick with the schedule for starting and quitting in order to respect their commitments. I tell them that the team will stay after the meeting to talk with them should any returnees desire to do so.

The team members should be prepared to talk a bit about themselves. Those who have been away from the Church and returned should briefly share some of those experiences as they initially identify themselves as team members when introduced to the group. Those team members who have never left the Church should also share their experiences in the same way. It doesn't matter that they haven't left and come back; they should share why they have stayed, or if they have struggled. When the team members talk, it should appear to be natural and relaxed and not rehearsed and "canned." Never say, "I've been asked to share…" because it somewhat invalidates whatever is shared and sounds contrived and staged.

As people enter the room, the team members should greet them and make small talk before the meeting begins. You can give the early arrivers their paperwork right away so they can look through the information and get a head start, or you can wait until everyone is seated before handing out the paperwork.

The agenda should be strictly followed for the first meeting in order to control and manage the meeting content. However, it works best if the meeting flow looks seamless rather than referring constantly to an agenda. Returnees seem to feel more comfortable and open up more if the meeting is firmly controlled but doesn't look stiff and contrived. This can be a delicate balance. Without an agenda, it's almost impossible to maintain control and keep the meeting positive when there are some really angry attendees. I don't break the returnees into smaller groups even if the group is large because it's too easy to lose control. The likelihood of angry people taking over a smaller group is too high in the small-group format to take the risk.

The agenda should be strictly followed even if some returnees who aren't particularly angry want to veer off in various directions. One such example is if a few insist on talking about divorce and annulment issues. No matter how adamant and forceful they are, it's best to say you're not an expert in those areas and you will be happy to route them to the particular person in the parish that handles that issue. You can even offer to talk with them after the session that night, but insist that right now the group is going to continue with what is on the agenda for the evening. It doesn't really matter what the issue is that someone wants to deviate toward—never abandon the agenda because you will lose most of the rest of the group and it will make the meeting look disorganized and unprepared. It's much better to kindly and calmly address their concerns with a few words, tell them you're happy to talk with them after the session that night and/or put them in touch with someone in the parish, but right now—tonight—the group will be sticking to the agenda.

The purpose of having the returnees complete the anonymous questionnaire is to allow them to vent on paper in a structured and controlled manner. The team members should also complete the questionnaires; this tends to make the returnees feel more comfortable.

During the discussion, the team members will be talking about their responses right along with the returnees. This helps to blur any distinctions of "we-they" between the team members and the returnees.

Never have team members obviously observe, monitor, and watch the returnees. Most of the returnees are walking on eggshells, skittish and nervous. To have team members "watching" them, "sizing them up," and evaluating them is entirely too intimidating and threatening for most returnees to handle. Some might leave almost immediately if they sense they're being studied like insects under a microscope. The team members should learn to blend in with the returnees, listening to them and trying to make them feel comfortable and at ease.

Agenda: Management Tool to Control the Meeting

1. Introduction/Prayer

The leader introduces him/herself and welcomes all attendees. Next, the leader says he/she's going to read the Prayer of Thomas Merton, and if they care to, the group can join in and read along or, if they're not comfortable doing so, they can just listen. The Prayer of Thomas Merton follows:

My God, I have no idea where I am going. I do not see the road ahead of me. I cannot know for certain where it will end. Nor do I really know myself, and the fact that I think I am following your will does not mean that I am actually doing so.

But I believe that the desire to please you does in fact please you. And I hope I have that desire in all that I am doing. I hope that I will never do anything apart from that desire.

And I know that if I do this you will lead me by the right road, though I may know nothing about it. Therefore, I will trust you always though I may seem to be lost in the shadow of death. I will not fear for you are ever with me and you will never leave me to face my perils alone.

After reading the prayer, explain that Thomas Merton was a modern-day Trappist monk who was involved in ecumenism with Eastern religions and that he died in the 1960s. He's written a number of books and is a popular author. I always mention how I feel his prayer speaks to all of us, but especially returning Catholics, because it describes how the Lord is with each of us, guiding us, even when we're not aware of his presence.

I tell them that just as the Prayer of Thomas Merton indicates, every one who is present at the meeting has been brought here by the Holy Spirit, and as we hear some of the stories from those present, the guidance of the Holy Spirit will be confirmed when we see all of the different paths that everyone traveled to be here. In the same way Jesus the Good Shepherd left the ninety-nine sheep to seek out the one who was lost, Jesus has sought out every one of them and brought them here. We know it took a lot of courage for them to call and to walk in the door, and we're glad they're there.

Explain to the group that in order to respect the privacy of all who are present, everyone should regard the content and conversation of the meeting as confidential and not to be shared outside the group. Many people who have been away from the Church have a church story and beneath it a big bundle of hurts. Talking through our church stories or faith journeys frequently helps us to deal with other issues in our lives. Be sure to explain that the group is not going to deal with specific issues and problems such as sex abuse or alcohol and drug problems. Accordingly, group members with these concerns should go to those specific counselors or groups that deal with those particular issues.

I go on to tell the group that Catholics Returning Home was started because the Church wants to invite all those who have left the Catholic Church to come home. Many people might think they're not welcome, even excommunicated, but in truth they're all invited to return. All the Church rules and regulations are still in place, and if some people have questions about divorce and remarriage, they can work through those concerns with our parish staff who handle such issues. Though certain issues and obstacles may seem overwhelming, there is nothing a returnee can't work through with the help of the Lord.

I then ask the team members to introduce themselves. They should each take a minute or two and say their names, welcome those who have returned, mention if they themselves have been away and returned (or if not, mention why they choose to be a part of the Church and note some of the struggles they've had). Perhaps team members will want to mention what they do for a living and/or in what other parish activities they participate.

After introduction of the team members, the team leader explains that the sessions are informal and that attendees will have a chance to ask questions and learn about what the Church is like today throughout the coming sessions. Hand out the list of team member's names, addresses, and phone numbers and encourage the returnees to call when they have questions or concerns.

Hand out the schedule of what will be covered over the next six weeks. Tell the returnees they have no obligation to attend each session but that it will help their progress if they do commit to regular attendance. If they do miss a session, they're more than welcome to attend the next series and repeat any or all of the sessions. Some people have attended off and on for years, which is fine because as there are always new people in the group, the sessions are always somewhat different.

Hand out the sign-in sheet (see page 60) for them to fill out their names, addresses, and phone numbers. Explain that they are under no obligation to sign-in. Since this sheet will be typed and handed out next week, they can call each other if they want to. If a member doesn't want their name and/or phone number handed out, they should say so on the sign-in sheet. It's really important for the team to know how each returnee found out about the sessions, so that the team can improve its outreach publicity. Also, having the names and phone numbers of the group members helps the team communicate with the returnees in case a meeting changes. The returnees will not be officially registering with the parish at this time. If they want to register with the parish, they will need to contact the parish office.

Distribute any parish bulletins, booklets, and pamphlets that pertain to parish activities and scheduled services. Tell them about *Handbook for Today's Catholic* (or a similar guide to Catholic beliefs, practices, prayers, and integration of the Faith into one's daily life) and *Returning Home to Your Catholic Faith*, which is a compassionate invitation and guide for their return (see page 106). Some parishes give the booklets away, but my feeling is that it's important for returning Catholics to learn responsibility in small ways by making commitments along the way such as paying a token amount for a Catholic guide booklet. I also encourage returnees to get a Bible and read the psalms and the gospels, especially chapter 15 of the Gospel of Luke, which contains the parables of divine mercy. I tell them that when I started reading the Bible, I got a children's Bible for children of all ages because it gave me a place to start. A good children's Bible has all the stories that a regular Bible does, and it's referenced to a regular Bible so that the reader can start at a level where they're able to understand, and later can move on to a more technical level.

Hand out the open-ended anonymous questionnaire (see page 58) along with pens/pencils and allow the group 10 to 15 minutes to complete them. Inform the group that the questionnaires are anonymous—they shouldn't put their names on them. Mention that expressing their feelings on paper is a healing step, and many returning Catholics have a lot of questions, concerns, and feelings of guilt. Let the returnees know that the group will discuss the questionnaire that night and before the returnees leave their questionnaires will be collected. The responses from the questionnaires will be compiled by the next session and distributed to the returnees so they can see how similar their questions, concerns, and feelings are to everyone else's. They're not alone.

2. Completing the questionnaire

After 10 to 15 minutes, when it looks like most are finished completing the questionnaire, the leader informs the returnees that the group is going to talk about the responses given on the questionnaires. Assure the returnees that they do not have to share their comments if they do not want to because there are always plenty in the group who want to talk and share. The leader starts out with the first question and says, "I am here because…" and explains a bit why he/she is here." Next, each of the team members answer that same question. At this point, the leader and team members can share more about themselves, for example, how they came to be a part of this ministry.

Next, the team leader asks if anyone else would like to share their response to question #1. Again, assure the group that no one should feel put on the spot. The leader can start going around the room in order, passing over the team, because they have already responded. For those returnees who are hesitant, pass them by, and go on to the next returnee. Usually, some of the returnees want to share. Let each one answer the question. Notice that we are channeling and managing the discussion down a path where we are eliciting certain information from the returnees. Some of the more angry returnees that might be there may try to jump in and dominate the discussion, ranting and raving on unrelated topics. The team leader has to listen very carefully, and allow some venting, but if a returnee gets too far off the path, the team leader will have to make a judgment and gently but firmly return the discussion to the matter at hand, which is answering question #1. Some strategies are to thank the returnee for sharing and then say, "We're going to get back to the discussion and let some others have a chance to participate." If someone tries to interrupt or change the topic, the team leader can say, "No, we're not talking about that topic right now. See me later if you like, but right now, we're going to talk about this topic."

Give everyone a chance to talk about question #1. Then repeat the procedure for question #2. Again, first let the team leader and each of the team members answer the question. Then, go around the room and ask each and every one of the returnees to share their response to question #2. Repeat the same procedure for all of the questions. In all the years I've done this program,

I've never made it through an entire questionnaire during the first session.

3. Optional: Profile Sharing or Video

Instead of discussing the entire anonymous questionnaire in #2 above, you can plan to break off that discussion and either show the video "An Invitation, With No Strings Attached" or with one of the team members sharing their story of being away and returning for about 10 to 15 minutes. Some of the stories are so touching and moving that they are very effective in helping the returnees bond and feel comfortable and among peers with the group. The team member who shares should be able to tell their story in a relaxed, natural manner without notes. Don't say "I've been asked to…." Instead, be able to simply talk about your experiences without looking like it's "canned" or rehearsed. Returnees seem to open up more if the discussion and sharing is more free flowing and natural.

4. End the session on time!

The leader should tell the group that the session is ending out of respect for everyone's time and commitments. If anyone wants to stay afterward, the team will remain for a while. Anyone who needs to leave can leave now or after our closing prayer. If anyone wants to join us in our closing prayer, they're welcome to do so.

5. Closing prayer

If the meeting room is in or near the church, I prefer to gather around the altar for the closing prayer. My current home parish has the meeting rooms upstairs in the church, so our group can easily walk down to gather around the altar. Gathering and praying around the altar might at first seem rather inappropriate for returnees; however, it has a profoundly positive impact on them. They can't believe they're worthy enough to be invited to gather around the altar. You can see the peace and tranquillity on their faces at being gathered and included in such a prayer. If the meeting room isn't in or near the church, then just gather around the table in the meeting room. Start out by gathering around either the altar or the table, ask all who care to participate to join hands, and pray the Our Father together.

After praying the Our Father, the team should remain for a while to answer questions and talk with those returnees who have specific questions and concerns.

6. Follow-up

After the first meeting and throughout the six-week series, the team leader and members of the team should call all of the attendees and offer to answer any questions they may have. The returnees really appreciate the individual attention, and some people seem to be more comfortable talking individually than in a group. These individual conversations are where the returnees have the opportunity to ask open-ended questions and seek help with their personal situations.

Initial "Anonymous" Questionnaire

Don't put your name on this!

Date: _____

1. I am here because:

   _____

   _____

2. My hopes/expectations in being here are:

   _____

   _____

3. My fears/apprehensions about being here are:

   _____

   _____

4. My feelings about the Church are:

   _____

   _____

5. My feelings about God at this time are:

   _____

   _____

6. The questions/issues I most want answered in these sessions are:

   _____

   _____

Other comments:

   _____

   _____

Agenda/Meeting Schedule

(Insert Parish Name)

Catholics Returning Home
Meeting Schedule

(Date)

(Location)

SESSION 1
Welcome/Overview of Series

SESSION 2
Sharing Stories of Faith

SESSION 3
The Church Today, Q & A

SESSION 4
Explanation of the Mass, Q & A

SESSION 5
Explanation of the Sacrament of Penance

SESSION 6
Creed: What Catholics Believe

Sign-In Sheet

Catholics Returning Home

Date: _____

NAME	ADDRESS	PHONE #	HOW DID YOU FIND OUT ABOUT THESE SESSIONS?
1.			
2.			
3.			
4.			
5.			
6.			
7.			
8.			
9.			
10.			
11.			
12.			
13.			
14.			
15.			
16.			
17.			
18.			
19.			
20.			

SESSION #2

Sharing Stories of Faith

Items to have on hand and things to do before the session starts:

- Recommended: Order video, "Stories of Faith From Catholics Returning Home" (see page 101)
- Have VCR and TV set up and ready to go
- The same two to five team members from the first week
- Name tags for team and attendees
- A comfortable, easy-to-find meeting room with a table and chairs
- Signs and greeters should be outside directing people how to find the meeting room to help any newcomers
- A candle and lighter
- A box of tissues
- Pens/pencils for attendees
- A list of team members, including phone numbers
- Copies of the Prayer of Thomas Merton
- Schedule for the six-week series showing topics by week
- Blank initial anonymous questionnaires
- Copies of compilation of anonymous questionnaires
- Sign-in Sheet
- Copies of *Handbook for Today's Catholic* to be available for returnees (see page 106)
- Copies of recent parish bulletins and any other information about parish activities
- Copies of *Returning Home to Your Catholic Faith* by Sally Mews, published by Liguori Publications. I recommend this book for returnees, because it is a compassionate invitation and guide for their return to the Church which parallels the sessions (see page 106).
- Handouts on specific Catholic issues such as annulments, divorce/remarriage, and so on

- Optional: Prerecorded background music and/or beverages and snacks
- Optional: Invite leaders from the divorced/remarriage and bereavement ministries to attend the meeting and introduce themselves to the returnees if they were not present at the first session.

During the first week, the focus is on the personal stories of the group and the related sharing and venting. During the second week, the focus shifts from those stories within the small group to the Church at large. The video "Stories of Faith From Catholics Returning Home" works very well to make that transition. The transition allows the returnees to be listened to, affirmed for their experiences, and aided in letting go of those past disappointments and hurts. By viewing the video and relating it to their own stories, they are able to acknowledge that others as well as themselves have been disappointed or hurt by the Church, that the Church is filled with imperfect human beings who make mistakes, and that it's time to move on and let go of any past disappointments or hurts instead of staying stuck in anger or resentment. The discussion is managed by having the returnees relate their stories to those seen in the video. In this way, they're being guided along a specific path of discussion so they don't go off on tangents.

The team welcomes the returnees back for the second week as they arrive. The compilation of the anonymous questionnaire can be handed out to each person as they arrive or when everyone has gathered together. Either way works. If there are new attendees, give them copies of the blank anonymous questionnaire and have them complete it and also give them copies of the team listing, schedule of the upcoming sessions, and any other paperwork that has already been given to the others. Offer copies of *Handbook for Today's Catholic* and *Returning Home to Your Catholic Faith* to those returnees who are interested.

The leader introduces him/herself and welcomes all the attendees including the newcomers. Next, the leader says he/she's going to read the Prayer of Thomas Merton (see page 51), inviting everyone to join in and read along. If anyone feels uncomfortable praying aloud, they are welcome to simply listen.

Just as they did in the first session, the team members introduce themselves to the group. This is helpful for newcomers as well as those who were there the previous week in bonding with the team members.

The leader discusses the anonymous questionnaires that were handed out at the previous session and reviewed by the team. The leader mentions that many of the responses are very similar, showing that we're not alone in our search for the Lord and our way back to the Church. The leader should comment only on common themes within the questionnaire, such as the fact that everyone in the group is searching and trying to find their way home and their own place in the Church. The returnees should be informed that they are united in this journey with those in the Church who are involved in the same ongoing search—this is one of the comforts of being part of the Church. The leader should not offer to answer all questions. If people ask questions, answer them only if they fit into the general idea of welcoming. Otherwise, tell them the team will talk with them after the session or call them on the phone to answer questions.

Next, the team leader introduces "Stories of Faith From Catholics Returning Home." The most important parts of the video are the actual stories as told by the returnees. Tell the group they should pay close attention to these narratives and try to relate some part of their own life stories to them because that's what the group will talk about next.

After viewing the video, the team leader makes a few comments about how the stories chronicled in the video relate to his/her own life story. Next, each team member relates the video to their own story. The team leader then goes around the room and asks each returnee to relate the video to their lives. If any of the returnees get off track, firmly bring them back to the video and their own lives. If they have unrelated comments or questions, offer to talk with them after the meeting. For the sake of control, be certain not to break the members up into smaller groups.

The discussion process of the first and second sessions allows returnees to vent and let go of any pent-up anger and hurt they hold toward the Church. One can see the change in the returnees each week as they become more comfortable and happy within the group and the Church.

Try to end the session by 9:00 P.M., stopping the discussion around 8:50 P.M. in order to have time for the closing prayer. Gather around the altar if possible, hold hands, and invite the group to pray the Our Father.

All the team members should stay afterward to answer any questions "held over" from the earlier session.

SESSION #3
The Church Today:
Changes Since Vatican II

Items to have on hand and things to do before the session starts:

- Have either a presenter scheduled or a thirty-minute video on Vatican II and the Church today
- Suggested optional video is "Vatican II: A Civilization of Love" (see page 101)
- Have VCR and TV set up and ready to go if using a video
- The same two to five team members from the first week should be there
- Preferably the group is meeting in a comfortable, easy-to-find meeting room with a table and chairs
- A candle and lighter
- A box of tissues
- Name tags for team and attendees
- Pens/pencils for attendees
- A listing of team members, their phone numbers
- Copies of the Prayer of Thomas Merton
- Schedule for Catholics Returning Home six-week series showing topics by week
- Copies of compiled questionnaire responses
- Sign-in Sheet
- Copies of *Handbook for Today's Catholic*
- Copies of *Returning Home to Your Catholic Faith*. I recommend this book for returnees, because it is a compassionate invitation and guide for their return to the Church which parallels the sessions.
- Copies of recent parish bulletins and any other information about parish activities, handouts on other Catholic information, such as annulments, Vatican II and the Church today, and so on

- Optional: Prerecorded background music and/or beverages and snacks

The team leader reads the opening prayer composed by Thomas Merton (see page 51) and invites others to join along if they care to. The team leader introduces the presenter or, if no presenter is available and a video is being shown, the team leader gives a brief explanation of the Second Vatican Council, saying it was the twenty-first Roman Catholic ecumenical council. Convened by Pope John XXIII, and conducted from 1962 to 1965, the Council's sixteen documents redefined the nature of the Church, gave bishops greater influence in Church affairs, and increased lay participation in the liturgy.

The presenter first provides some personal background information about him/herself including what they do for a living and how they got involved with Church ministry. Next, he/she gives an overview of Vatican II, the changes since the Council, and takes questions on related topics. The presentation should be approximately forty-five minutes, followed by questions, answers, and discussion. The speaker may prefer to use a video rather than a prepared presentation.

The content of the presentation should employ simple, basic terms at a grade-school level of understanding. Always use simple rather then complex terms. Remember to treat returnees like children in adult bodies. A simplified, general, historical overview of the Church from the Council of Trent to the Second Vatican Council to the present day is an important step for returnees as they come to understand where the Church has been and how it has come to be where it is at this point in history.

Topics to address regarding differences in the Church following the Second Vatican Council might include:

1. The development of "Bible study" groups
2. Diaconate (back to roots)
   a) Baptism
   b) Weddings

  c) Funerals

  d) Service to community

3. Lay ministry

  a) Leadership roles in ministry

  b) Volunteer as well as paid employees

  c) Parish and arch/diocesan leadership

4. Lay involvement in liturgy

  a) Eucharistic ministers

  b) Contemporary Mass

  c) Liturgy Commission

  d) Lay involvement in organization of the liturgies

  e) Laity—decorating the altar

  f) Lectors

5. Confession to reconciliation

  a) Life orientation vs. laundry list of sins

  b) Face to face vs. behind the screen

6. Mass

  a) Local language

  b) Removal of Communion rail

  c) Priest faces congregation

  d) Congregational participation

At the conclusion of the session, call the group together for the closing prayer. Join hands and pray the Our Father. (Pray around the altar if possible.)

SESSION #4

The Mass

Begin with the Prayer of Thomas Merton (see page 51) for all who care to participate. If you have secured a priest to give a "walk-through" presentation of the Mass, introduce him and explain his role at the session before giving the group over to him. If a priest has not been secured for the session, you can either watch a thirty-minute video on the Mass or have someone other than a priest give a presentation and explanation of the Mass. A question-and-answer session related to the Mass can follow. If a priest is not available and no one on the team feels confident enough to explain the Mass, a thirty-minute video on the Mass will suffice. Suggested videos include: "A Video Guide to What Catholics Believe About the Mass" and "Liturgy" (see page 102).

The most important part of the walk-through Mass or explanation of the Mass is to connect or relate to the returnees and help them feel comfortable and at home in church and with the Mass. Use basic, grade-school terms. Try to use humor throughout. Fr. Ron Folger, currently an associate pastor at St. Peter's in Antioch, Illinois, does a terrific job of putting the returnees at ease by giving a down-to-earth explanation of the Mass. For example, in his presentation, Fr. Ron will say that the pall—the cloth-covered piece of cardboard that covers the chalice—was originally used to keep the bugs out of the wine and the Communion rail was used to keep the animals back because the community would bring produce and animals as offerings. The "washing of hands" was done because the priest handled all sorts of "offerings."

These suggestions are in no way meant to be disrespectful toward the Mass. Rather, they are merely a suggestion for presenters to help them with some "icebreakers" in their presentation. Most presenters have so much heavy-duty theology floating around in their heads that it is almost impossible for them to translate it to a grade-school level of understanding. The result is that returnees are blown away by all the technical terminology and become too intimated and afraid to ask questions for fear of showing their ignorance. Such higher-level presentations result in distancing returnees rather than making them feel at ease. The best presentations I've seen are those where the presenter explains the Mass in a basic manner.

My current pastor, Fr. Pat Cecil, does a terrific job of relating to returnees at their level. He gathers them into the sacristy and shows them all the nooks and crannies and where things are stored. He takes out all the vestments and explains all the different colors. As he "suits up" in the vestments, he explains to them what all the differences are. Watching him in action with the returnees is indeed a treat. He gathers them around him, I think, the way Jesus did with the little children. He draws them close to him around the altar and you can see them gravitate toward him. He explains the pieces of cloth on the altar and he shows them where the relic is encased.

He goes through the entire Mass, in very simple terms, stopping periodically to ask if there are any questions. Finally, he holds hands with them and leads an impromptu closing prayer that ends with the Our Father. It's a work of love in action. The returnees greatly enjoy this experience and frequently list it as one of the high points of the Catholics Returning Home series.

If a video of the Mass is used instead, the team leader should show the video and then follow that by leading a discussion and question-and-answer session regarding the viewing. The closing Our Father should be led around the altar (if possible) for all who care to join in.

SESSION #5
Explanation of the Sacrament of Penance/Confession

Begin with the Prayer of Thomas Merton (see page 51) for all who care to participate. If you have secured a priest to give a "walk-through" presentation of the sacrament of penance, introduce him and explain his role at the session before giving the group over to him. If a priest has not been secured for the session, you can either watch a thirty-minute video on the sacrament or have someone other than a priest give a presentation (see outline, pages 71–72). A question-and-answer session related to the sacrament can follow. If a priest is not available and no one on the team feels confident enough to explain the sacrament of penance, a thirty-minute video on the Mass will suffice. A suggested video is "A Video Guide to What Catholics Believe About Reconciliation" (see page 102).

The presentation should be approximately forty-five minutes, followed by questions, answers, and discussion. The approach should be pastoral rather than theoretical or dogmatic. Many people who have been away from the Church are petrified of the sacrament of penance. They're afraid they're going to be yelled at. Many have been away for years and don't even know where to begin in trying to remember what they've done or not done.

Some folks have suggested we offer the sacrament of penance to the returnees during this session. I have tried having a priest available to them for the sacrament on an optional basis, but it wasn't very well received. Instead, many felt coerced and pressured into going to confession. Accordingly, I don't recommend offering penance during the series but instead letting the returnees follow through on their own.

One Catholics Returning Home team was very upset with the new associate pastor's presentation of the sacrament of penance. The newly ordained priest gave a very detailed and lengthy explanation of the various types of sins and related punishments. He told the

group of the necessity of confessing every sin. One frustrated returnee asked how he could do that since he had been away for over
thirty years. The priest told this man that he should break down the
confession into detailed ten-year increments! Another Catholics Returning Home team from a different parish spoke of their frustra-
tion with their priest's presentation on the sacrament of penance.
He spent a lot of time discussing various types of sins, emphasizing
the necessity of confessing all the details.

At one parish where I led the Catholics Returning Home ministry, after the explanation of the sacrament of penance, I told the returnees they could make an appointment with the various priests at
their convenience or go during the regularly scheduled times that
penance was offered. Then, in order to help them to know which
priests to ask for, I named and described the various priests and told
them what they were like. When I described one of the priests, I said,
"He's a very nice fellow who's hard of hearing and he doesn't wear
his hearing aid." Needless to say, most of the returnees went to that
priest for penance!

The presentation of the sacrament of penance should include:

- Handouts of the examination of conscience and any other
  information on the sacrament of penance (see page 72)
- An overview of the current form of the sacrament of penance
- Emphasize the differences between pre- and post-Vatican II
  perceptions of the sacrament of penance; that is, laundry
  list of sins vs. maintaining a life orientation toward loving
  God, self, and others.
- Mention the parable of the Lost Sheep (Lk 15:4–7) or the
  parable of the Prodigal Son (Lk 15:11–32) and their common theme that all sins can be forgiven.
- Let the returnees know that it will not be expected at their
  first confession that they will have to remember and con-
  fess everything for all the years while they were away, but
  they should focus their attention on those sins they can
  recall at this time.

- Questions and answers for the presenter.
- Show the returnees the confessional (or reconciliation room) and explain how it is used. In my experience, the returnees love to look it over.

Close this session with a prayer. Invite everyone to gather around the altar (if possible) and pray the Our Father.

Examination of Conscience

1. Find a quiet place to sit or kneel.
2. Review your life—those things you have done and those things you have not done for which you are sorry.
3. Reflect on the Ten Commandments. To the best of your memory, call to mind any sins against the commandments. Is my heart centered on God, or do I worship things (money, power, and so on) that are less than him? Do I keep holy the Sabbath? Do I seek to speak only the truth, and avoid gossip and slander? Do I seek to promote the values of life and battle against those forces that threaten the innocent? Have I taken something that did not belong to me?
4. Reflect on Jesus' commandment to love your neighbor as yourself (Mt 22:34–40). Do I truly love my neighbors? Do I ever use my neighbors as a means to an end? Do I contribute to the happiness of my family? Do I aid the poor and unfortunate? Do I seek to promote peace and understanding in race relations? Have I been compassionate and merciful to those who have wronged me? Have I allowed fear and anxiety to keep me from acting with love towards others?

SESSION #6
Wrap-up, Evaluation, and Discussion of the Creed

Items to have on hand and things to do before the session starts:

- The same two to five team members from prior sessions
- The same comfortable, easy-to-find meeting room with table and chairs
- A candle and lighter
- A box of tissues
- Name tags for team and attendees
- Pens/pencils for attendees
- A listing of team members, their phone numbers
- Copies of the Prayer of Thomas Merton
- Copies of the Nicene Creed/Explanation of Creed
- Blank evaluation forms
- Schedule for current and next Catholics Returning Home six-week series, showing topics by week
- Copies of *Handbook for Today's Catholic*
- Copies of *Returning Home to Your Catholic Faith*
- Copies of recent parish bulletins, information about parish activities, and handouts on such topics as annulments

The purpose of the final session is to close out the series, affirm the attendees for participating, and assure them they are on a lifelong journey which is only just beginning. In addition, the attendees are asked to complete an evaluation form and invited to become involved with the returning-Catholics ministry. Lastly, the Nicene Creed is discussed and explained in an effort to help the returnees become more comfortable with their faith.

As people enter the room, the team members should greet them and make small talk with them before the meeting begins. You can give the early arrivers their paperwork right away so they can look through the information and get a head start, or you can wait until they're all seated before handing out the paperwork to everyone.

The agenda should be strictly followed for the final meeting in order to control and manage the meeting content. Again, it works best if the meeting flow looks seamless rather than referring constantly to the agenda. Returnees seem to feel more comfortable and open up more if the meeting is firmly controlled but doesn't feel stiff and contrived. As mentioned earlier, the reason for the strict control is to keep a couple of really angry people from wresting control of the meeting and dominating and monopolizing the evening. By the last session, however, most of the attendees have become more comfortable and friendly.

The leader introduces him/herself and welcomes all attendees. Next, the leader says he/she's going to read the Prayer of Thomas Merton (see page 51), and everyone is welcome to read along, though if they're not comfortable doing so, they can just listen.

Just the Beginning

The leader informs the returnees that although this is the last session, it's still only the beginning of their journey with the Church. They're welcome to come back for the next series and bring someone else too. At this point, ask the returnees to complete the evaluation form (see page 80). Explain that the input from these forms will help future returning-Catholics teams improve the program. Returnees will also be asked if they would like to help with the future Catholics Returning Home programs, even though they are most likely doubting how they could be ready to help others return when they've just walked in the door. Ask them to remember how comfortable and at ease they felt when they heard other team members share their experiences of being away and returning to the Church. In the same way, they can help themselves and others by being willing to share their own stories. Really encourage them to consider being involved and on the team. Distribute the evaluation form and ask them to complete it. Give them about ten minutes to complete the evaluation and then collect them.

Distribute any additional parish information such as bulletins, booklets, and so on that describes parish activities and scheduled services. Encourage them to check out the other ministries in the parish, especially Bible study and other small-group activities. Tell them the team members will be happy to help them "get connected" in any of these other ministries if they need help. Mention again the Liguori books, *Handbook for Today's Catholic* and *Returning Home to Your Catholic Faith.*

The Nicene Creed and Explanation

Distribute the Nicene Creed/Explanation sheet (see pages 78–79) and tell the returnees that in continuing their journey in the Church it's time to think a bit more about what they believe. The Nicene Creed is the foundation of what Catholics believe and this is the night the group is going to discuss the Creed. Ask the group to look at the sheet that shows the Creed and its explanation. Next, go around the room in order and have each person read a phrase and its explanation. Then, that person can make a comment, ask a question, relate it to their own lives, or attempt to define it in their own words. In my experience, some of the most profound and touching beliefs have been expressed by returnees in this format.

At one group, we had a pair of women who were really not connecting with the process throughout the series. When we got to the last evening and the discussion of the Creed, I handed out the Creed/Explanation sheet and told them we would be discussing and reflecting on it in order to help them roll it around in their minds and understand it in greater depth. At this point, one of the women said that she couldn't discuss the Creed since it had too many big words and she lacked the proper religious education. She was indignant that I was even asking her to do such a thing. However, she said that even though she wasn't qualified to discuss the Creed, she would take the last line which said "Amen, so be it" because she believed it with all her heart! All of us in the room were taken aback by her great expression of faith. She didn't have to say anymore than that, because what else could be said? She had said it all!

It's critical that the leader control and manage the discussion by systematically going around the room and having each person read, reflect, and comment on one segment at a time. As each person does that, the leader must "moderate" the discussion so that it doesn't go off on tangents. It's fine to say that much of the Creed is a mystery and accepted by faith. Throughout the discussion, I interject key points, such as the Catholic belief on the "final coming of Jesus." Many returnees have expressed fear about the "end times" and whether the end of the world is coming soon. I always say that Catholic belief is that we're not to worry about the day or hour, because no one knows when it will be. We are not to live in fear, but instead to live in faith as if each day is our last. If anyone goes off on a tangent, firmly bring them back to the discussion at hand. Always offer to talk with them after the session or to call them and try to put them in touch with parish staff if you can't answer their questions.

Saying Good-Bye

End the session on time! Thank the returnees again for attending, invite them back for the next series, and encourage them to bring others back. The leader should tell them that the group is ending the session on schedule out of respect for everyone's time and commitments. If anyone wants to stay afterward, the team will be there for a while. Anyone who needs to leave can leave now or after our closing prayer. If anyone wants to join in our closing prayer, they're welcome to do so.

After praying the Our Father, the team should stay for a while, answering questions and talking with returnees. Some of the returnees will not want to leave, especially after the last session. This is a great accomplishment. It's better to have them want more than to drop out because they feel the series has run too long. I find that the plan outlined in this book for a returning-Catholics program works best at six weeks in duration. Some members may want it to go on longer. Help these "graduates" of the program channel their energies by directing them to other ministries or schedule some special adult education/small-group updates for them as well as others in the parish for the Spring or the Fall.

Nicene Creed	Explanation
1. We believe in one God.	*Three Persons—One God*
2. The Father, the Almighty, maker of heaven and earth, of all that is, seen and unseen.	*First Person of the Trinity; Creator of all that which is known or unknown.*
3. We believe in one Lord, Jesus Christ, the only Son of God, eternally begotten of the Father, God from God, Light from Light, true God from true God, begotten, not made, one in Being with the Father. Through him all things were made.	*Second Person of the Trinity; Son, Redeemer; this tells us his relationship to the first Person; the Son is equal to the Father.*
4. For us men and for our salvation he came down from heaven: by the power of the Holy Spirit he was born of the Virgin Mary, and became Man.	*The second Person of the Trinity took on humanity in the person of Jesus.*
5. For our sake he was crucified under Pontius Pilate; he suffered, died, and was buried. On the third day he rose again in fulfillment of the Scriptures; he ascended into heaven and is seated at the right hand of the Father.	*Summarizes the paschal (Easter) mystery. We recall this at Mass during the memorial acclamation. Jesus rose from the dead, body and soul; he returned to the Father as Jesus, second Person of the Trinity, human and divine.*

Nicene Creed	Explanation
6. He will come again in glory to judge the living and the dead, and his kingdom will have no end.	*The Second Coming of Christ. The Final Judgment at the end of time.*
7. We believe in the Holy Spirit, the Lord, the giver of life, who proceeds from the Father and the Son. With the Father and the Son he is worshiped and glorified. He has spoken through the Prophets.	*Third Person of the Trinity; Sanctifier; relationship to the first and second Persons of the Trinity; equal with the Father and the Son; source of inspiration for the Scriptures.*
8. We believe in one holy catholic and apostolic Church.	*United in creed, code, and worship. Holy because Jesus is holy. Universal, founded on the apostles.*
9. We acknowledge one baptism for the forgiveness of sins.	*Initiation into the Body of Christ.*
10. We look for the resurrection of the dead, and the life of the world to come.	*We will also rise from the dead, body and soul, like Jesus. Eternal life—heaven or hell.*
11. Amen.	*"So be it!" Statement of affirmation and acceptance.*

Catholics Returning Home—Evaluation Form

1. What did you like about the series?

   _____

   _____

   _____

   _____

2. Suggestions for improving the series?

   _____

   _____

   _____

   _____

3. Would you be willing to participate in the ministry as follows:

   ❏ Participating on planning team?

   ❏ Attending ongoing sessions and sharing your story?

4. Other comments:

   _____

   _____

   _____

   _____

Name: _____

Address: _____

Phone #: _____

CHAPTER 6

Follow-Up Sessions and Ongoing Support

~

The most important aspect of any returning-Catholics program is the small-group faith sharing and storytelling. Those returning are able to relate, bond, and be accepted by program team members in a small-group faith community. By sharing their faith journeys, the returnees are able to let go of their fears and failures and develop trust within the parish community. Only then are they ready, willing, and open enough to seek and accept updated information about Catholic Christianity.

Some parishes have changed the program to cut out the first two weeks of small-group faith sharing and instead focused only on the four-week update and information portion. In my experience, this omission is a big mistake since it doesn't give returnees the chance to "tell their stories" or verbalize their pent-up distrust and possible anger. Their wounds can never heal without the ability to have those negative experiences acknowledged. Through acknowledgment, affirmation, and acceptance, they can finally let go of those past hurts and disappointments and move on.

The catechetical content of the prototype program is designed to be an update of the basics of Catholicism for adults taught at a grade-school level. Many returnees left as teenagers or young adults and never acquired an adult understanding or appreciation of their faith. The six-week series is designed to welcome them back, help them overcome their difficulties with the Church, facilitate development of trust in the faith community, and then update them on the basics of Catholicism in order to help them reconnect and feel comfortable.

Much is accomplished in that six weeks in order to move people from being totally disconnected from the Church to feeling comfortable and at home with a working knowledge of the basics. Most of the returnees say they want the series to continue beyond the six weeks. However, I recommend leaving it at the basic six weeks, otherwise you'll deter new people from attending because it would be perceived as being too long. A miracle occurs in the attendees in the space of six weeks. They grow and develop in their faith life to the point that they are hungry for more. It's critical that graduated returnees be channeled to other ministries in the parish where they can continue their journey of faith development. They should be included on the mailing lists for upcoming adult-faith offerings.

Recommended ministries for ongoing support and enrichment include those for the divorced/remarried, annulment process, bereavement, Bible study, and other small-group faith communities. It's good to offer an annulment seminar on a regular basis. Some parishes offer a two-evening series on annulments once or twice per year. The first evening is on the general annulment process and the second evening covers the specifics. These seminars are usually very well attended and should be opened up to the entire parish rather than just the graduates of the returning-Catholics program.

Many graduates are interested in becoming involved in the Catholics Returning Home ministry and other ministries. Be sure to make available an index of the various parish ministries that lists the names of the contact persons. Returnees feel wanted and part of the parish family if they become personally involved with the Church in some way. In addition, some returning-Catholics teams periodically call past attendees and maintain contact with them, answering any questions they may have and providing a much-needed "life line" to the Church.

CHAPTER 7

Publicity

~

P ublicity is the key to recruiting for any returning-Catholics program. The number of attendees corresponds directly with how
well the publicity gets out. The methods of publicity that I've selected are relatively easy to use and inexpensive. Publicity should be
started six weeks before the series is set to begin and continued until
the day the first session begins. After the program has finished, a
bulletin announcement should inform the congregation of the number of attendees who returned.

The publicity methods include a listing on the parish Web site,
bulletin announcements (including surrounding parishes), bulletin
inserts, inserts in parish mailings, flyers sent to parents of PSR and
school children, brochures, prayers of the faithful, commentator and
presider announcements, news releases published in the religion section of newspapers, outdoor signs on parish grounds and/or
parishioner's businesses, and free announcements on radio and cable
television. In addition, the team can place flyers in stores, libraries,
and other businesses.

Outdoor signs are very effective. Keep the wording on the signs
simple because you have just a few seconds to grab your target
market's attention. The more complex the sign is, the fewer phone
calls you'll get.

The sample bulletin announcements, flyers, and prayers of the
faithful that follow have been used and are quite effective. The samples
here serve as a "time saver" so that you don't have to re-invent the

wheel. However, you are encouraged to write your own personalized announcements over time so that you have some variety.

A tri-fold brochure is highly effective. To save money, you can ask a funeral home to sponsor and pay for the brochure, allowing them to put their advertisement on the back. A lot of funeral homes are very eager to sponsor such efforts because most other Church activities avoid having a funeral home as a sponsor. Also, placement of the brochures in the funeral homes is a great place for publicity because you touch a lot of people that are searching and don't normally see the inside of a church.

Outdoor Signs

On Parish Grounds and/or
Parishioners' Businesses

Catholics Returning Home

Begins Soon

call xxx-xxx-xxxx

(Insert parish name)

Announcements Before or After Mass

We are asking each of you to make a special effort to ask any of your nonpracticing friends, relatives, or acquaintances to attend our Catholics Returning Home series beginning (insert date, meeting location). See the bulletin announcement for more information.

Or:

We are asking each of you to make a special effort to ask any of your nonpracticing friends, relatives, or acquaintances to join us for (select Lenten/Holy Week/Easter/Advent/Christmas) services. We invite them to attend our Catholics Returning Home series beginning (insert date, time, location). See the bulletin announcement for details.

Or:

Our parish family is delighted that those of you who do not worship regularly with us chose to be with us for this (Lenten/Holy Week, Advent/Christmas, Sunday celebration). Please note the special announcement in the bulletin for the series entitled "Catholics Returning Home" which is for people who are away from the Church.

Or:

We welcome returning Catholics who are here to worship with us today. We have a special program called "Catholics Returning Home" for nonpracticing Catholics who may be considering a return to the Church. This program begins (insert start date). For more information, see details in the bulletin.

Announcement by Presider Before or After Mass or During Homily

For those who have been away from the Church for whatever reason, we're delighted that you are here. We invite you to attend a special series called "Catholics Returning Home," beginning (insert start date). Please see the bulletin for details.

Prayers of the Faithful

For all those who have drifted away from the Church that we may be signs of the Lord's love and care for them.

That all who are separated from the Church may come to possess the great joy of knowing God's compassionate love and acceptance.

That those returning to the Church to celebrate with us during this (Lenten/Easter or Advent/Christmas) season may be blessed with a renewal of faith and a closer walk with the Lord.

That those who are troubled and separated may find peace in the sacrament of penance and at our parish celebrations during this holy season.

For those who have left the Church, that the Lord's compassionate love will lead them back.

For those who accepted our invitation to return home to the Church, that they may be blessed with a renewal of faith and a closer walk with the Lord.

Bulletin Articles

Catholics Returning Home

Do you know someone who has left the Church? Most of us do not have to look very far to find nonpracticing Catholics in our circle of family and friends. Many of us are concerned about these loved ones, but we don't know how to help them. Obviously, most of them are searching, but how can we help them find their way home?

As baptized, practicing Catholics, we have a precious gift of faith and love from the Lord that needs to be shared with our nonpracticing brothers and sisters. First, we need to pray for them. Next, we need to extend a personal invitation to them to come home to the Catholic Church. Most nonpracticing Catholics are waiting for an invitation to return. Many mistakenly think they are excommunicated and are not welcome to return for a variety of reasons.

Many nonpracticing Catholics carry with them a tremendous amount of guilt and misinformation about the Church and are afraid of approaching the Church for fear of being rejected. You can make a tremendous difference in someone's life simply by reaching out to them and telling them that we miss them and would like for them to come back home to our Church family.

Here at (insert parish name) we have a special program to help nonpracticing Catholics return to the Church entitled "Catholics Returning Home." The next series begins (insert start date, place, and time). Please pass this article on to anyone who might be interested. For more information, call (insert Catholics Returning Home coordinator's name, phone number, and e-mail address).

Or:

Catholics Returning Home

(Insert parish name) will offer a six-week series entitled "Catholics Returning Home" beginning (insert start date, time, and place). The sessions are for nonpracticing Catholics who are seeking answers to questions about returning to the Church. If you know someone who has left the Church, please invite them to join us. For more information, call (insert Catholics Returning Home coordinator's name and phone number).

Or:

Have You Drifted Away From the Church?

Are you angry with the Church or God? Please give us a chance to listen to you and address your concerns. Join us for our informal weekly sessions beginning (insert start date, place, and time). The meetings will be facilitated by former nonpracticing Catholics who you may find share many of your feelings. In the meantime, if you have any questions, please call (insert Catholics Returning Home coordinator's name and phone number).

Or:

An Invitation to Nonpracticing Catholics

The Church has changed and you may not know it! Has it been a while since you've been to church? Are you mad at the Church or God? Please give us—and yourself—another chance. Join us for informal sessions for nonpracticing Catholics. We would like to know your feelings and try to address your questions.

The meetings will be held at (insert time and place) on six consecutive (insert day) evenings beginning (insert start date). If you have any questions in the meantime, please call (insert Catholics Returning Home coordinator's name and phone number).

Or:

Get Rid of Those Negative Feelings!

Have you been hurt or angered by the Church? There are others who may share many of your feelings. Please give the Church and yourself another chance by joining us at six weekly sessions on (insert day) evenings at (insert time and place) beginning (insert start date). Former nonpracticing Catholics will share their stories and listen to your feelings and concerns. There is no obligation, and perhaps some of your questions will be answered. For more information, please call (insert Catholics Returning Home coordinator's name and phone number).

Or:

Catholics Returning Home

We are happy to report that we have had numerous calls from people seeking answers to questions about returning to the Catholic Church. Many have been attending our meetings over the last several months on (insert day) evenings at (insert time and place). These are people of all ages who have been away from the Church. Our next series begins (insert day, start date, time, and place). We would like to invite anyone who is interested to join us. Please call (insert Catholics Returning Home coordinator's name and phone number) for more information.

Or:

Catholics Returning Home

Have you been away from the Church for a while? Have you ever thought about returning? If so, we would like to welcome you back to (insert parish name). We have a special ministry for people just like you who have been away from the Church. Please join us for a six-week series that begins (insert day, date, place, and time). We would like to address your questions and make you feel at home once more in the Catholic Church. For more information, please call (insert Catholics Returning Home coordinator's name and phone number).

Or:

Catholics Returning Home

Were you raised Catholic but do not come or seldom come to church anymore?

Are you a Catholic who now feels separated from your church?

Would you like to know more about the Catholic Church as it is today?

Would you like to feel at home in the Catholic Church again?

No matter how long you have been away and no matter the reason, we invite you to consider renewing your relationship with the Catholic Church.

Date: (insert start day and date)

Time: (insert time)

Place: (insert parish name and place)

For more information, call (insert Catholics Returning Home coordinator's name and phone number).

Or:

Catholics Returning Home
An Invitation
for Nonpracticing Catholics

Were you raised Catholic but do not come or seldom come to church anymore?

Are you a Catholic who now feels separated from the Church?

Would you like to know more about the Catholic Church as it is today?

Would you like to feel at home in the Catholic Church again?

No matter how long you have been away and no matter the reason, we invite you to consider renewing your relationship with the Catholic Church. Please join us for informal listening sessions and an update of the Catholic faith. The sessions are held at (insert start day, date, time, and place). For more information, call (insert Catholics Returning Home coordinator's name and phone number).

Flier and Full-Page Bulletin Insert

Catholics Returning Home

(Insert year/season) Schedule

(Insert date)
Welcome
Overview of Series
Sharing by Team and Attendees

(Insert date)
Sharing Stories of Faith
Discussion and Sharing

(Insert date)
The Church Today: Changes Since Vatican II
Explanation of Major Changes—
Mass in English, Lay Involvement, Bible Study

(Insert date)
Walk-Through of the Mass
(Along With Explanation and Historical Overview)

(Insert date)
Explanation of the Sacrament of Penance (Confession)

(Insert date)
The Creed: What Catholics Believe

Or:

Catholics Returning Home
An Open Door for Returning Catholics

(Insert parish names)

Welcome!

Were you raised Catholic but do not come or
seldom come to church anymore?

Are you a Catholic who now feels separated
from the Church?

Would you like to know more about the Catholic Church
as it is today?

Would you like to feel at home in
the Catholic Church again?

No matter how long you have been away and
no matter the reason, we invite you to consider renewing
your relationship with the Catholic Church.

(Insert dates and six-week schedule of topics
as listed in the flier above)

Sponsored by the (insert area name) Catholic Parish

Brochures

This brochure could be paid for and sponsored by funeral homes. Funeral homes often look for good causes to sponsor but so many groups shy away from having them as sponsors. By giving funeral homes space on the back of the brochure for their advertisement, they will provide the financing for printing fees, and these funeral homes are always willing to put the brochures out in their own facilities where many returning Catholics visit when they attend funerals. In this way, the publicity is getting out to those who are away from the Church.

Wording for the Brochure:

Catholics Returning Home
An Invitation to Nonpracticing Catholics

Welcome!
(Name of parish)
Catholic church welcomes you home.

If you are a Catholic who has been away from the Church for a while, this invitation is for you. Our faith community misses you and is incomplete without you. No matter how long you have been away, and for whatever reason, we invite you to consider renewing your relationship with the Catholic Church.

Please join us for informal listening sessions and an update of the Catholic faith facilitated by former nonpracticing Catholics. The sessions are conducted in a support-group format. Everyone is welcome, no matter where they are from.

Catholics Returning Home Schedule

Catholics Returning Home is a six-week series held three times a year: Come Home for Easter; Come Home for Christmas; and Come Home in the Fall. The six-week series includes:

Week 1: Welcome, Overview of Series, Faith Sharing
Week 2: Sharing Stories of Faith
Week 3: The Church Today: Changes Since Vatican II
Week 4: Explanation of the Mass
Week 5: Explanation of the Sacrament of Penance
Week 6: Explanation of the Nicene Creed

For details call (Insert address and phone number of parish and contact person).

Please pass this on to anyone who would be interested.

(Insert Mass schedule)

Parable of the Lost Sheep: Which one of you, having a hundred sheep and losing one of them, does not leave the ninety-nine in the wilderness and go after the one that is lost until he finds it? When he has found it, he lays it on his shoulders and rejoices. And when he comes home, he calls together his friends and neighbors, saying to them, "Rejoice with me, for I have found my sheep that was lost." Just so, I tell you, there will be more joy in heaven over one sinner who repents than over ninety-nine righteous persons who need no repentance.

—Gospel of Saint Luke 15:3–7

Newspaper Press Release

These news releases should be sent twice to all the local newspapers—about six weeks and three weeks before the sessions start—to be printed in the "religion" sections. Since they are printed without charge, the newspapers have the right to edit them. Thus, I suggest keeping the press release brief, noting only the bare essentials of the program. Be certain to include contact information.

Catholics Returning Home

(Insert parish name, address) will conduct an ongoing series called Catholics Returning Home on six consecutive (insert day) evenings at (insert start time and place) beginning (insert start date). These sessions are for nonpracticing Catholics who are seeking answers to questions about returning to the Church. There will be informal sharing and an update of the Catholic faith. For more details, call (insert Catholics Returning Home coordinator's name and phone number).

Television and Radio Spots

Note that both television and radio stations often have their own specific forms that must be completed so as to arrange a free public service or charitable, nonprofit announcement. Submit both versions so that you're giving them a choice of having a longer or shorter notice depending on the space allotted rather than allowing them to "edit or shorten" the notices themselves. Be sure to request that your announcements not be edited, and to include contact information for the television and/or radio stations.

Catholics Returning Home

(Insert parish name, address) will conduct an ongoing series called Catholics Returning Home on six consecutive (insert day) evenings at (insert start time and place) beginning (insert start date). These sessions are for nonpracticing Catholics who are seeking answers to questions about returning to the Church. There will be informal sharing and an update of the Catholic faith. For more details, call (insert Catholics Returning Home contact person's name and phone number).

Catholics Returning Home

Nonpracticing Catholics are invited to informal listening sessions and an update of the Catholic faith. This six-week series begins (insert start date and time) at (insert parish name and city). For details, call (insert Catholics Returning Home contact person's name and phone number).

Chapter 8

A Final Word
of Encouragement

~

Many years ago when I was discerning the call to undertake a ministry to returning Catholics I did a lot of soul searching because I didn't think I was worthy or good enough to serve God in this capacity. Who was I? Just an ordinary laywoman. What did I know about the doctrine of the Catholic Church? Who would listen to me? I struggled with a poor self-image and scrupulosity. My limited experience with the Catholic Church as a young, abused child had left me with a very warped and distorted image of God and the Church. I thought God was an ogre who kept track of every mistake I made. I was sure that he was ready to send me to hell for the least infraction of "the rules." I agonized and split hairs worrying about whether or not I had committed various sins and whether or not I could ever be forgiven. My perception of God and the Church was one of control and fear.

When the Lord touched my heart and life with his healing love, my fear was gone. A miracle occurred and I was set free. I became a new person with an intimate, personal, and loving relationship with the Lord. My life was forever changed and transformed. I was at peace with myself and others and I wanted to share that experience with everyone. I knew so many others who had also drifted away from the Church, who were confused and struggling as I had been. It bothered me a lot that the Church wasn't doing something to help all those who were adrift. I decided that somebody had to do something, and the Lord helped me see that I was the "somebody" who could make a difference.

On the one hand, I was painfully and acutely aware of all the reasons why I shouldn't get involved with this type of ministry, such as family and professional responsibilities, lack of theological or educational training, and the fact that I was just an "ordinary layperson" and not a priest. Finally, I decided that I could either focus on all the reasons why I wasn't qualified and do nothing towards starting this ministry or I could do the best I could knowing that it would never be perfect. I might make some mistakes and many people may not like or appreciate what I was doing, but if I helped even one person return to the Church and become reconciled and at peace with themselves, God, and others, then all my effort was worth it.

Since that time, the Catholics Returning Home program has grown and spread all over the world and there have been many who have returned and had their lives changed forever for the better. I have been privileged to see many make this transition in their lives. It is indeed nothing short of glorious. It is an honor and a gift to be allowed to witness this profound transformation in so many lives. Everyone I know who has been involved in this ministry—be it team leaders, priests, or deacons—says the same thing. They too are grateful and graced by being part of this wonderful work of the Lord. I know that you will be too!

Sources for Programming

Videos

Chapter 5, Session #3
THE CHURCH TODAY: CHANGES SINCE VATICAN II
Optional Videos:
Vatican II in History
Forty Years Later
For prices and ordering information, contact
Hallel Institute at 800-445-7477 or www.hallelvideos.com.

Chapter 5, Session #4
THE MASS
What Catholics Believe About Mass (598985)
For price and ordering information, contact
Liguori Publications at 800-325-9521 or www.liguori.org.

Liturgy
For price and ordering information, contact
Hallel Institute (see above)

Chapter 5, Session #5
EXPLANATION OF THE SACRAMENT
OF PENANCE/CONFESSION

What Catholics Believe About Reconciliation (598923)
For price and ordering information, contact
Liguori Publications at 800-325-9521 or www.liguori.org.

Chapter 6
FOLLOW-UP SESSIONS AND ONGOING SUPPORT

What Catholics Believe About RCIA (917983)
What Catholics Believe About Other Religions (917990)
What Catholics Believe About Prayer (917969)
What Catholics Believe About Rights, Freedoms,
and Responsibilities (917976)
What Catholics Believe About Lifestyles (917952)
What Catholics Believe About DVD Set: The Sacrament
Collection (DV900)

For prices and ordering information, contact
Liguori Publications at 800-325-9521 or www.liguori.org.

Laity
Evangelization
Ecumenism
Religious Freedom
After the Council

For prices and ordering information, contact
Hallel Institute (see page 101)

Books, Bulletins, Web Resources

Books

Catechism of the Catholic Church, United States Catholic Conference, Double-day, 1995.

Catholic Answers to Fundamentalists' Questions, Philip St. Romain, Liguori Publications, 1984.

The Essential Catholic Handbook, A Summary of Beliefs, Practices and Prayers, A Redemptorist Pastoral Publication, Liguori Publications, 2004.

Faith for the Future: A New Illustrated Catechism, Liguori Publications, 1998.

The Gift of Sex: A Christian Guide to Sexual Fulfillment, Dr. Clifford and Joyce Penner, Penner Books and Tapes, Pasadena, CA (626-449-2525 or www. passionatecommitment.com), 1981.

Handbook for Today's Catholic, A Redemptorist Pastoral Publication (also available in Spanish), Liguori Publications, 2004.

Returning Home to Your Catholic Faith: An Invitation, Sally L. Mews, Liguori Publications, 2003.

Vatican Council II: The Conciliar and Post Conciliar Documents, Austin Flan-nery, O.P., Costello Publishing Company, Northport, New York, 1992.

While You Were Gone: A Handbook For Returning Catholics, William J. Bausch, Twenty-Third Publications, Mystic, CT, 1994.

Bulletins

Catholic Update articles on various topics by St. Anthony Messenger Press (28 W. Liberty St., Cincinnati, OH, 45202, 800-488-0488, www. americancatholic.org/newsletters/CU.aspx).

Support Groups/Web Sites

American Association of Pastoral Counselors, 9504A Lee Highway, Fairfax, Virginia, 22031-2303; Phone: 703-385-6967; http://aapc.org. The AAPC provides and promotes theologically informed, spiritually sensitive, ethically sound, and clinically competent counseling and consultation as an extension of the ministry of faith communities. The AAPC is an excellent resource for those returnees in need of professional assistance in dealing with past hurts and future healing.

Catholics Returning Home Resources: www.catholicsreturninghome.org, Returning Home to Your Catholic Faith by Sally L. Mews, 2003. A compassionate invitation and guide for those returning to the Church (see page 105).

WEORC, 1528 West Glenlake, Chicago, IL 60660-1826; www.marriedpriests.org. A like-to-like ministry that provides counseling, support, and assistance in finding employment for former religious making the transition back to secular life.

Letter of Understanding and Agreement

Your use of the Catholics Returning Home program, name, and logo "Catholics Returning Home: A Ministry of Compassion and Reconciliation (CRH)" by Sally L. Mews acknowledges your agreement to abide by the following requirements:

(1) CRH is copyrighted; thus Sally L. Mews owns all rights in the program and content. Additionally, CRH is recognized and approved by the USCCB (United States Conference of Catholic Bishops) in "A Time to Listen…A Time to Heal," which is a directory of model programs for reaching out to nonpracticing Catholics. Thus Sally L. Mews wants to maintain ownership rights and the integrity of the CRH name and program.

(2) CRH is time-tested and proven; thus it is to be used in its entirety as designed. Please do not change the content, design, or name of the CRH program.

(3) If you make substantial changes to CRH and create your own program, then please do not use the CRH name or logo. In this instance, if you "draw" from the CRH program, your creation must be substantially different in content, design, and name so as not to be confused with CRH. In addition, you should acknowledge your source as being from CRH.

(4) Please let Sally L. Mews know if you have any questions or comments concerning the use of CRH.

(5) If you would like to use the CRH logo, please contact Sally Mews at ssmews@comcast.net.

SALLY L. MEWS
FOUNDER/DIRECTOR OF CATHOLICS RETURNING HOME

Other Related Liguori Publications Titles

Returning Home to Your Catholic Faith
An Invitation
Sally L. Mews

Returning Home to Your Catholic Faith addresses with honesty and compassion the fears, hurts, and guilt that many inactive Catholics feel when they first consider returning to the Church. A brief, to-the-point presentation of issues always stress God's mercy; most people who leave and later return do so as part of the process of maturing. Practical tips on how to reconnect with the Church are included. The section on what the Church is like today is a reassuring overview of the opportunities available in a parish.

ISBN: 978-0-7648-1099-2

Catholics Continuing the Journey
A Faith Sharing Program for Small Groups
Sally L. Mews

This six-week program, originally designed to help people grow in their faith after returning to the Church, is an excellent reflection tool for any study group in the parish setting. Each session lasts approximately 1-1/2 to 2 hours and follows the theme: "What is your image of Jesus?" It is an appropriate study course for any time of the year and its emphasis on group dynamics makes it an easy and effective way to build community among parishioners.

ISBN: 978-0-7648-1503-4

Handbook for Today's Catholic
Revised Edition

Handbook for Today's Catholic is presented in easy-to-understand language, with content divided into Beliefs, Practices, Prayers, and Living the Faith, and is also fully indexed to the *Catechism of the Catholic Church*. RCIA and parish adult faith formation groups, high school religious education classes, inquirers into the Catholic Faith, and anyone who wants to have the essentials of Catholicism at their fingertips will welcome this affordable faith resource.

ISBN: 978-0-7648-1220-0

To order visit your local bookstore or call 800-325-9521 or visit us at www.liguori.org